Michael Alexander is the pseudonym of a nurse who has previously worked in the UK and New Zealand.

CONFESSIONS OF A MALE NURSE

Body parts that came off in his hands. Teenagers with phantom pregnancies. Doctors unable to tell the difference between their left and their right. Violent drunks. Singing relatives. Sexism. And more nudity than the sex industry . . . Michael Alexander never knew what he was getting himself into. But now, sixteen years since he first launched into his nursing career — as the only man in a gynaecology ward — he's pretty much dealt with everything . . .

MICHAEL ALEXANDER

CONFESSIONS OF A MALE NURSE

Complete and Unabridged

CHARNWOOD
Leicester

First published in Great Britain in 2012 by
The Friday Project
An imprint of HarperCollins
London

First Charnwood Edition
published 2014
by arrangement with
HarperCollins
London

A catalogue record for this book is available
from the British Library.

ISBN 978–1–4448–1908–3

Published by
F. A. Thorpe (Publishing)
Anstey, Leicestershire

Set by Words & Graphics Ltd.
Anstey, Leicestershire
Printed and bound in Great Britain by
T. J. International Ltd., Padstow, Cornwall

This book is printed on acid-free paper

For my wife and kids

Disclaimer

The stories described in this book follow my progression from an inexperienced nurse to a relatively effective professional. To protect confidentiality, some parts are fictionalised, and all places and names are changed, but nonetheless they remain an honest reflection of my experience working as a male nurse over the past 16 years — surprising as that might come to be!

Contents

Who am I?

I am just your everyday, run-of-the-mill nurse, with a unique story to tell. Okay, unique is not *quite* accurate; anyone that spends time working in healthcare has their own uniquely similar stories. Every day we come into contact with people from all walks of life, from the destitute to the wealthy, the young to the elderly, simple to genius, cruel to caring.

Though I never planned on being a nurse, caring for others was in my blood: my great-grandfather was a medic through two world wars, and my mother was also a nurse. Medicine provided them with a living, and so at the wholesome age of 17 I figured it would be good enough for me; nursing meant a guaranteed job. Little did I know that nursing would prove to be so much more than just a way to make a living.

Now, 16 years on, I'm still working in healthcare. I wouldn't be if I didn't like caring for others, but I'm only now realising that nursing isn't just about what I can do for others; nursing is also good for me. Everyone likes that warm feeling they get when they help someone. Well, I *really* like it, and especially when I've done that little bit extra.

Looking after others is all I've ever known. I've seen people in all states of health, both mentally and physically, and I have come to the conclusion that our bodies themselves are the greatest equalising factors in our inglorious existence. Now, I want to show you what it's like, what it takes, and what really goes on in the front line of the caring profession.

Why do I want to do this? On the positive side, I want to tell you just how amazing your average nurse really is; I want to prove that a good nurse can literally be the difference between life and death. On a more negative note, this is my chance to make up for the times when I should have spoken out about some of the horrendous goings-on in many hospitals, but didn't; times when I kept quiet, because of fear, ignorance, or simply being at a loss about what to do.

Introduction

There is one thing almost all of us are going to be at some point, and that is a patient. One day, most of us are going to need to depend on someone when we are at our weakest. That someone is most likely going to be a stranger and that stranger is most likely to be a nurse.

I have worked with patients suffering from dreadful diseases, some of which I had never even imagined, let alone dealt with, like Guillain-Barré syndrome or motor neurone disease, or horrific cancers that spread through the body. Now, after 16 years, I've done pretty much everything — from keeping someone comfortable while their body is failing and the pain is getting too much to cope with, to chasing a confused (and very naked) patient down a corridor. I've learnt how to deal with a family who have been told their loved one is not going to make it (which never gets any easier, regardless of whether it is expected or not). I've experienced my fair share of emotions: frustration, impotence, despair, at the unfair ways disease and misfortune can strike those most deserving of life; at other times, relief when someone's suffering ends.

But no matter how much I sympathise, I don't really know what it is like to be a patient. I have only seen things from a nurse's perspective, where you can't afford to get *too* emotional or involved. I often wonder what it must be like to be on the other side, to be lying in bed, to see things through a patient's eyes.

The only way I have of imagining is to use my experience of the way people in the past have reacted to being in my care.

What I have noticed, is that a person's behaviour generally changes as soon as they become a patient. Some people become extremely nervous, which is understandable, and may explain why some pretty silly questions are asked. *Does surgery mean I will have to have an operation?* Then, there are the people who, during a ward round with their consultant, will nod as if in understanding, but when the doctor leaves they haven't the faintest idea what is going on. I've heard many a patient, when asked by their consultant, 'How do you feel?' respond by saying that they feel fine, when in fact they'd spent the morning complaining about their ailments.

Some people suddenly find they are unable to do simple tasks for themselves, like pour their own water or fluff their own pillows, even if they are physically quite capable. Others become so used to being in hospital that they know how a ward runs better than some of the staff. Some become so demanding that no matter how many of their requests are satisfied, they will never be happy, while others are so grateful for any small service — even just spending five minutes listening to them — that they want to shake your hand or marry you off to one of their grandchildren. I've seen people too afraid to disturb the nurse, as they don't want to be a burden, even though they are worried about the pain in their chest. I've seen others treating nurses like servants. Then there are people who lose all initiative, because they aren't sure what they are supposed to do; they don't know how to be a patient and they're not sure what exactly a nurse's role is.

When I picture myself sitting for hours in the waiting room, seeing patients who came after me being dealt with first, I wonder whether this would irritate me, or whether I'd be calm and rational, like all nurses want their patients to be. Then when I finally get called through to see the doctor, I imagine expecting the doctor to have all the answers to my problems as, 'Doctor knows best.'

It must be frightening for patients who are admitted to be put on a drip, to have blood taken every day, or tubes stuck in some surprising places. For some having to share a room with a bunch of sick strangers might seem difficult.

But that's why I'm here, your average nurse. It isn't just about giving you your medicines and dressing your wounds. I'm here to explain things, including the foreign language the doctors use. I'm here to help you in and out of bed, to help you help yourself. I'm here to help calm you in the night when you wake up wondering where you are, or worrying about that pain in your chest. I'm here to help make your treatment as bearable as possible.

I

Slippery beginnings

Did I always know what I was doing? Of course not, but I couldn't tell the patients that. A nurse must be confident and assertive, yet caring. The problem was I didn't feel confident, nor the least bit assertive; I did care, though.

I will never forget my first day at Allswell, a hospital situated in the middle of nowhere — well, maybe more like everywhere. Allswell was a fairly typical example of all that is good, bad, outrageous and hilarious about hospitals across the civilised world. I remember vividly the reaction as I walked into the ward and explained I was the new nurse; mouths dropped open and there were mutterings of 'there must be some mistake' and even 'this is a joke'. The nurse in charge of the ward even made a phone call to the head of personnel to explain the problem. You see, I was not just straight out of college; I was the only male in a gynaecology ward. The most important people I met that first day were Sharon and Cherie. Sharon was the nurse in charge of running the ward, similar to a traditional Matron. Cherie was the nurse whose job it was to familiarise me with the ward. It was a huge responsibility for her, although I didn't realise it at the time. Over the next two months, Cherie's task was to transform me from a naïve new graduate to an effective, safe and efficient member of the team. I don't think either of us knew how difficult that was going to be.

My first day was spent following Cherie around. I was introduced to every patient and shown where everything was: the fire escape, cardiac arrest alarms, cardiac arrest trolley, treatment room, sluice room. I was handed a three-inch-thick folder of policies and instructed in the use of the computers, admission and discharge procedures.

All I really wanted to do was get my first patient and see if I could do the job. I went home that first day forgetting everything Cherie told me.

★   ★   ★

My third day on the job and I still didn't feel the slightest bit at ease. In fact, I was feeling worse. Driving to work each morning, my mind was in overdrive thinking of the things that could go wrong, of all the ways that I could stuff up, and today I was getting my first patient.

'I'm going to give you Mrs Stewart,' Cherie said to me. 'She's day one post an abdominal hysterectomy. It will be good experience for you.'

Before starting on the ward the only time I had to think about a uterus was in the class studying anatomy books, and now here I was helping a patient recover from having one of the most intimate parts of her womanhood removed.

Forty-three seemed quite young to be having a hysterectomy, but at least Mrs Stewart already had three kids, so hopefully she wouldn't feel too bad about her surgery.

'Good morning, Mrs Stewart,' I said, as I walked in the door. 'I'm your nurse for the day. How are you feeling?'

Even hooked up to an infusion of narcotics, her shocked expression made it clear that the last person Mrs Stewart expected to see in a gynaecology ward was a male nurse.

She soon got over her shock. She had other things to worry about, such as the tubes sticking in her arm, the urinary catheter, and an abdomen that had been sliced open and sutured up.

'I don't know. How should I feel?' she asked me. 'I can't feel anything. I'm numb from the stomach down. I had prepared myself for some pain.' She sounded almost disbelieving.

'It's the miracle of the epidural,' I replied, trying to sound knowledgeable, without actually having the faintest clue as to how effective epidurals normally are.

'Well it's amazing. I never thought I would feel this good. I wish I'd had this when I had my kids.'

I nodded my agreement and kept silent; there really wasn't a lot I could say.

The shift seemed to go better than I'd expected, although this was probably due to the bright spirits of Mrs Stewart, as opposed to any particular skill on my part. Still, she didn't seem completely at ease in my presence.

'I can't wait to tell my husband I've had a male nurse looking after me.'

Mrs Stewart had made this remark at least a dozen times over the course of the day and it seemed a bit forced, almost as if she was still trying to convince herself that it was okay to have a male nurse. Never mind, I was sure she would feel better about it by tomorrow; at least, I hoped so, because tomorrow was going to be a lot more challenging, for her as well as me.

The next morning, Cherie informed me that Mrs Stewart was to have her epidural removed.

'It's pretty straightforward,' Cherie explained, 'just pull.'

I was expecting something a little bit more detailed, but 'just pull' sounded easy enough.

'Oh, and make sure you give her some analgesia straight after you take it out. You want to have something working before it wears off,' Cherie added, before heading off on her own rounds.

Epidurals are not something nurses learn about in detail, although they're pretty simple to follow. A needle is inserted between the vertebrae of the back, into the epidural space. The epidural space is a membrane that surrounds the spine. A plastic tube is threaded along the needle and into this space. The needle is removed, while the plastic tube is left in place and an infusion of analgesia is slowly pumped. This keeps the patient completely pain free from about the navel down.

All I had to do was 'pull' the tube out.

Thankfully, Mrs Stewart was philosophical about having the epidural removed.

'I'm not looking forward to the pain, but I guess it means I'm making good progress,' she said.

'Oh, don't worry, Mrs Stewart. We'll give you some medicine before the epidural wears off. You'll be fine,' I said, as I picked up her drug chart.

She seemed comforted by my words. I looked at her drug chart to see exactly what sort of analgesic I could give, but decided it would be better to ask Cherie. As Cherie was the nurse guiding me, she was the person I was to go to with any problem, no matter how big or small.

'We usually give a Voltaren suppository,' Cherie answered when I asked her. 'It's long-lasting and tends to work really well. You've given one before, haven't you?'

I *had* given one before, but only to a male patient. Somehow, during my student training I had managed to avoid having to go near women's private parts. I explained this to Cherie, and her face brightened with a smile.

'Well, there's not much difference. You can't go wrong.'

I wasn't so sure.

The epidural was removed under Cherie's supervision and it really was as simple as she had described, a slight 'tug' and it was out, no resistance, no trouble. A bit of iodine and a transparent dressing and everyone was happy. To make the most of a good opportunity (that is Mrs Stewart held on her side by Cherie and her bottom facing me) I prepared to give the suppository.

'Stop,' Cherie said, as I had one hand on Mrs Stewart's upper cheek, while the other hand was ready to do the deed.

'What's wrong?' I asked, frantically trying to think what I had done wrong.

'Aren't you forgetting something?' Cherie asked me.

Under pressure my mind remained a blank.

'The jelly — the lubricant — you forgot to put some on your finger,' she said, in a slightly exasperated tone of voice.

'Oh, yeah right, sorry,' I replied, as I squeezed the tube of jelly a little too hard. So hard that I managed to lather up not just my finger but both of my hands as well. Cherie rolled her eyes but kept silent.

I hadn't even begun to insert the suppository because with my rubber gloves soaking in lubricant I was struggling to hold up her cheek with one hand and the suppository in the other. The cheek kept slipping down and covering the target. I looked up to see an amused (and slightly bemused) looking Cherie.

'Let me help,' Cherie said as she grabbed hold of Mrs Stewart's cheek and held it up.

'Here we go, Mrs Stewart,' I said as I went for gold.

I heard Cherie stifle a gasp. I suddenly felt nauseous.

With far too much lubricant on my hands, the suppository had missed and gone in the wrong hole. At least Mrs Stewart didn't seem to notice anything because she was still numb from the remains of the epidural.

'I've never seen that happen before,' remarked Cherie.

I looked up into her face and gave her a 'What now?' sort of look.

She made a hooking gesture with her finger.

'You must be kidding,' I mouthed back at her. There was no way I was going searching in 'there' — it even crossed my mind that 'searching' in 'there' could be a form of abuse. My only hope was that it hadn't gone too far. One thing I was sure of was that Voltaren was pretty rough on the stomach, and I began to worry what it could do if left in such a sensitive place.

I needed to move fast because this felt wrong. I looked up at Cherie again and shook my head. There were some things a man should not do and this was one of them. But Cherie motioned for me to hurry up and get on with it.

'You're a nurse now,' Cherie whispered quietly, as if this meant I had an open licence to dig around in women's private parts.

Eventually, I took a deep breath and with a quick flick of my index finger I managed to scoop out the offending suppository. Cherie gave me a 'thumbs up'. I quickly popped the thing in the right spot, while Cherie rolled Mrs Stewart back on to her back.

'All done, Mrs Stewart,' I said. 'How do you feel?'

Mrs Stewart took a moment to answer. She gave me a strange look.

'Fine,' she said eventually.

I left the room very quickly, without saying another word.

'You won't tell anyone, will you?' I asked

Cherie back in the nurses' office. 'I felt like a total pervert,' I added.

Cherie didn't answer, because she was bent double laughing — although she eventually recovered long enough to inform the whole ward.

Sharon's law

A nurse is a nurse first, and a woman (or in my case, a man) second. At least, that was the thinking of my mentor, Cherie. One of Cherie's favourite sayings was, 'If a woman has to go down there, then so do you.' Maybe that was why she made me go after that suppository. In Cherie's world of nursing, there was no gender, just doing the job and doing it well. My problem was I never expected to be doing this particular job, in this particular area of nursing.

I had applied to work at the hospital as a general nurse on the new graduate programme. I expected to be offered a 'normal' nursing job in a surgical or medical ward. But I couldn't turn down the offer of a full-time job. They didn't even interview me for the position. Maybe the personnel manager was too embarrassed to admit that she had made a mistake. Maybe this was the reason no one seemed to like me, especially Sharon.

★ ★ ★

'Stop daydreaming: pull your finger out your arse and do some work.'

The calm way in which Sharon said this left me speechless.

'And close your mouth, you look stupid.'

Sharon seemed satisfied that she had made me

17

look the fool and moved on down the corridor in search of her next victim. Only four weeks into my nursing career and I was learning to avoid my charge nurse at all costs. I looked over at Cherie.

'I have to tell you something you won't like' — Cherie was never afraid to speak her mind — 'Sharon doesn't like you . . . a lot.'

With my self-esteem at an all-time low, I began to go about my rounds.

I knew that I knew nothing. It was a good thing really, as *too much* confidence can be harmful.

It won't come as a surprise that I struggled with some parts of the job already. Things were unfamiliar, and it was usually vitally important that I got them right. The latest problem in front of me was called erythromycin. It's an antibiotic, and in this case it needed to be injected straight into a vein.

'What are you waiting for?' Sharon asked me, as she entered the treatment room and saw me standing with a syringe full of intravenous antibiotic.

'I'm waiting for Cherie,' I replied cautiously.

Hospital policy stated that all intravenous medicines needed to be checked by a second person, but I felt a bit useless standing there doing nothing because mine had already been checked.

'Let's have a look. I'll check them for you.' Sharon began to look at the drug chart.

'It's already been checked,' I replied. 'I'm just waiting for Cherie, because she has to watch me administer it.' Again this was hospital policy.

Sharon rolled her eyes and quietly cursed. I'd said the wrong thing.

There was an awkward silence; a silence which I hoped would last, because I knew when Sharon spoke it wouldn't be to say how conscientious I was.

Sharon finally broke it with a calm voice, though I could sense the anger building:

'Are you a registered nurse?'

I wasn't sure whether to answer. Was it a rhetorical question? I knew there was more to come, so I just nodded my head.

'Well, start acting like one,' she added, her voice rising up an octave. 'You can't have someone holding your hand all the time. Take some initiative.'

I left the treatment room in a hurry and approached my patient.

Here I was standing at the patient's bedside, with a syringe full of antibiotic that I'd never given before. Policy stated that I needed three months' supervision before I could give these medicines on my own, and I was just nearing the end of my first month.

My mind was chaos turning over silly thoughts, crazy thoughts, even suspicious thoughts. Was Sharon trying to set me up to fail? What if something went wrong? I wasn't even aware of all that could go wrong. If something did happen, no one would back me. Sharon would deny everything. What could I do? I knew what I should do . . . but I couldn't risk facing the wrath of Sharon.

I slowly opened the intravenous valve and began to insert the syringe. In my nervousness I fumbled the syringe and it fell on to the bed. Was it still okay to use? I didn't know, but Sharon would kill me if she saw me drawing up another antibiotic. I inserted the syringe and gave the antibiotic, because it was easier to do this than create a scene. I watched the patient's chest to monitor her breathing. I felt her pulse . . . did it skip a beat? No, I was imagining things.

I waited anxiously those first few minutes, silently praying that nothing went wrong. Thank goodness my patient didn't know how nervous I was, but even more importantly, thank goodness she didn't have a clue that I wasn't supposed to be doing this yet, even if my charge nurse had ordered me to. After five minutes, I figured that if anything was going to happen, it already would have. The one thing that even new nurses know is that with intravenous medicine when something goes wrong, it tends to happen pretty instantaneously.

I'd got away with it, this time, but would I always be so fortunate? One month in and life as a male nurse was already proving to be a minefield.

The scapegoat

The words looked all the same. The handwriting was horrendous: this could only be the writing of a doctor.

'Can you make this out?' I asked fellow nurse Jen, handing her the medical notes.

'You're hopeless,' she responded in a tone of voice that seemed only half-joking. 'You need to take some initiative. There won't always be someone around to cover for you.'

Jen was yet to help me even once, and I would never ask her for help if there was anyone else around to ask.

'I'm not asking for much,' I replied, 'just some help interpreting the writing.'

As Jen tried to decipher the notes, I could see a frown forming. She was having as much trouble as I had been.

'It says colonoscopy. You do know what that is, don't you?' she asked, with more than a hint of condescension in her voice.

'If it's the long, flexible tubey thing, with a bright light that goes a foot or two up your butt, then I guess I do.'

I was just as surprised as Jen that those words had come out of my mouth. I was just a graduate, while Jen had at least 20 years' nursing experience behind her.

As I took the notes back, I avoided Jen's gaze, worried that I had gone too far.

I took another look at the writing. I wasn't 100 per cent convinced that it said colonoscopy. I knew she'd be pissed off if I asked her again, but I had to be certain.

'Are you sure about that, Jen?' I asked, increasingly regretting my earlier cheeky remark.

'I've been doing this job since before you were born,' she replied. I could see the veins begin to stand out on her forehead as she tried to control her anger. 'You need to listen to your betters, or you're going to mess up really bad one day.'

Now that I felt so positively reassured, I went ahead and got the patient ready for her colonoscopy.

* * *

'Are you sure I need to drink all this?' Mrs Knight asked me, after I had prepared the medicine for her to drink. At 79 years of age, Mrs Knight was quite a surprisingly sprightly little lady — a dedicated member of the local women's walking club. Unfortunately she was having some women's problems and had needed to be checked out.

'I'm quite confident,' I replied — trying not to put too much emphasis on the 'quite'.

But Mrs Knight was still unsure about drinking two litres of salty water, and her hesitation was making me doubt my instructions as well.

After I poured the first glass, I stayed to watch as Mrs Knight took a mouthful of liquid.

'Urrrgh.'

She almost choked. When her coughing fit passed, she looked me straight in the eye: 'I can't drink that stuff; there has to be another way. Besides, why do they want me to have an empty bowel? It's not my bowel that's causing the problem.'

She had a point and as I couldn't come up with any answer other than the nurse in charge told me to, I thought I had better check again.

'Mrs Knight's refusing to take the drink,' I began to explain to a very angry looking Jen, my voice tapering to a near whisper. 'She doesn't seem to think she needs it.'

Jen looked ready to hit someone. I held Mrs Knight's medical file in front of me like a shield. She grabbed the file and looked at the notes again.

I didn't see the look of shock that must have crossed her face, but I couldn't miss her outburst.

'You bloody idiot,' she yelled at me. 'What have you done? How much did you make her drink?'

Oh shit, what was wrong? All I'd done was what she'd told me to do.

'Not much, not much at all, not even half a glass,' I stammered. 'I was only doing what you instructed.'

Obviously this was my screw-up; Jen certainly wasn't going to take any of the blame.

'I said *colposcopy*. You don't know what a colposcopy is, do you?'

★ ★ ★

Thankfully, Mrs Knight didn't drink her two litres of bowel-cleaning liquid and she was sent for her colposcopy, which was a look up the front side, not the back.

I kept silent — embarrassed and fuming at the same time. Jen had definitely said colonoscopy, but it was my word against hers, a new grad against an old hand. I would not win this argument.

Every ward needs to have senior, veteran staff members around — that inexperienced people like me can turn to. I knew that Jen was a good nurse and could normally be relied upon to make the right decision, but sometimes impatience, being too busy, or even not liking a colleague can cloud a person's judgement. Thankfully, this is not too common.

This little piggy

After six months of putting up with a charge nurse that disliked me, and patients that looked at me as if I was from Mars, I had doubts about how much longer I could go on. But there were times when it all seemed worth it; times when I connected with a patient, and could physically see the difference I made.

'You seem to know a lot about wounds,' Sharon said to me one day.

Her comment caught me by surprise, because I really didn't think that I had any particular skill or knowledge about wounds.

'Not really,' I replied, trying to figure out if she was thinking of a particular patient that I had done a good job on. With my mind still a blank I came up with a rather non-specific reply, 'I just like to keep things simple; back to basics.'

She nodded her head as if I had said something wise. 'I've heard some good things about what you've been doing with Mr Mannering's feet. You're not afraid to do what needs to be done and I like that.'

I thanked Sharon for the compliment and went about my business, surprised and confused. This was the first time Sharon had ever said anything nice to me.

Mr Mannering's were by far the worst toes I'd ever had to dress. I couldn't help but wonder what Sharon was thinking when she said I'd done a good job with his feet. His toes were black, completely and utterly rotten. The dressing was doing nothing useful, although the gauze between the toes was helping them from sticking to one another. I was simply keeping the rotten things covered until he got his foot, or even whole lower leg, amputated.

Due to a bed shortage, Mr Mannering was the only male patient in the gynaecology ward, and he sat upon his bed like a king upon his throne: he had everything at his fingertips and everyone at his beck and call. His room had a television, radio, electric bed, a great view of the hospital rose garden, and, of course, his nurse call bell within easy reach.

'Has the newspaper arrived yet?' This was Mr Mannering's regular way of greeting me in the morning. I was never offended that he didn't say good morning or good to see you. Mr Mannering spent all day on his bed; the only time he left was to be taken in a wheelchair to the toilet or the shower. For Mr Mannering, the morning newspaper was very important: it was a key part of his daily routine and his way of staying in touch with the outside world.

The newspaper also proved to be a convenient tool for me, providing a useful distraction from what I was about to do next.

'Shall we get started?' I asked.

Mr Mannering looked up from his paper and gave me a nod.

Whenever it came time to change the dressing on his toes he always made the same simple request: 'I don't want to see them. I don't want

26

to be put off my breakfast.'

As well as using the newspaper as a diversion, I put a couple of pillows on his shins to act as a barrier, in case he looked up at the wrong time and caught a glimpse of his feet.

I placed a piece of gauze between his big toe and the next.

Mr Mannering had had problems with his feet and the lower part of his legs for five years. He was diabetic, and over time the diabetes had affected his circulation. As a result, he had been battling with leg ulcers, but things had suddenly come to a climax when his toes had turned black.

'Could you get us another cup of tea when you're finished down there? Oh, and some biscuits as well?'

'Yeah, just give me a moment, I should be finished soon,' I replied. As I tried to pry apart his rotten toes, the thought of food didn't seem quite right.

Mr Mannering chose this moment to inquire after his feet.

'So how's it looking down there?' he asked, almost nonchalantly, just as if he was asking about the weather.

'It's not looking good,' I replied. 'But at least it doesn't look any worse.'

There was no point being overly optimistic or pessimistic in my response, because no matter what I said, he responded the same way:

'Well, you seem to know what you're doing. I'll leave everything in your capable hands'

The little toe was the hardest to dress: it was

too small, so the dressing wouldn't stay in place.

I tried to pull his toes apart, so I could have another attempt at slipping in the piece of gauze.

Then . . . oops.

I could feel bile building up in the back of my throat. Somehow I managed to stop myself from vomiting, but I couldn't completely hide the sound of air being brutally forced up through my throat and out my mouth, as my stomach clenched.

'Everything all right down there?' Mr Mannering had lowered his newspaper and was looking me in the eye.

'You look awfully pale,' he added. 'Are you feeling okay?'

How did I feel? His little toe was resting between my fingers. I'd pulled it off. On the bright side, at least he wasn't bleeding, although the smell from the foul, yellow-green-black pus seeping from the stump was making my stomach lurch again.

'Well come on lad, speak up.'

For the first time in the two weeks that I had been doing Mr Mannering's dressings, I heard a note of concern in his voice. I thought of the words he had said a moment earlier: 'I'll leave everything in your capable hands.' I don't think he meant it quite so literally.

As I crouched at the end of the bed, unable to think of anything to say or do, I had a vision of holding up his toe and offering it to him.

'We have a slight problem,' I finally said. 'But it's nothing to worry about — really.'

Mr Mannering leant forward. 'What's wrong?'

'It's your toe; your little toe,' I began to explain. 'It's come off.'

'Come off, what do you mean come off? Toes don't just fall off.'

He had a point, toes don't generally fall off.

'Well, I pulled a bit too much and it just, well, came away in my hand,' I said.

Mr Mannering took a minute to collect his thoughts, while I was still kneeling at the end of the bed with his toe between my fingers.

As the silence grew, I tried to justify my actions in my head: *It really isn't my fault. His feet are rotten. He's going to get them chopped off anyway; surely he realises this.*

I looked at Mr Mannering's face to try to gauge his reaction. Then I heard a strange sound. It couldn't be ... but it was. Mr Mannering was laughing — a deep, throaty, contagious laugh. I found myself joining in.

'They're going to chop it off anyway, lad. You've just made their job a bit easier,' he said to me.

'Ever thought of being a surgeon?' he added and broke into another round of laughter, as if this were a great joke.

'Well, what do you want me to do with it?' I asked — the discussion finally coming around to practicalities.

'Well, I don't want it,' he said. 'Throw it in the rubbish.'

It didn't seem quite right throwing it in the bin — after all, it was a body part — but then again, a pretty gross part, so in it went.

Two days later, Mr Mannering went to surgery

and had not just his toes, or even his foot, amputated, but his leg from just below the knee.

Mr Mannering had been the first male patient I had worked with as a registered nurse, and it was as if I had seen a light of hope at the end of a long tunnel. I found myself not only comfortable working with Mr Mannering, but actually enjoying it. This was just as well, because my time in the gynaecology ward was nearly up. I had received word from management that, as part of the graduate programme, I was to be rotated to a general surgical and medical ward. I just had to survive one more week.

II

A glimmer of hope

Six months after graduation, I was moved to Ward 13. I knew from the very start that it was going to be challenging, but hopefully in a good way. It was a small hospital and space was at a premium. The ward had surgical patients, medical patients, and urology patients.

The surgical cases often involved abdominal and vascular surgery, as well as urology surgery, which is anything to do with the kidneys and their associated plumbing. While the medical patients were a mix of everything. It was only in the years to come that I would learn that this set-up was not very common (although it happened often enough because of a shortage of bed space). It was certainly not ideal, but one huge benefit of the situation for me was that I gained a whole lot of experience in a relatively short space of time. I began to see things truly from the perspective of a caregiver.

Who's to blame?

Horrendous, horrible things sometimes happen in my line of work. Things that make hospitals seem like a living nightmare. But good can come out of even the worst experiences, even if it is just a new way of looking at something — sometimes, perception is everything.

Interpretations of a situation can vary tremendously, especially when it comes to a patient's perspective versus that of a nurse. It's to be expected that the nursing staff will have a better understanding of health and illness and how the body deals with sickness. What is not always appreciated is a patient's understanding, or lack thereof, of a particular problem.

★ ★ ★

'Get ya hands off it; I don't want ya breaking anything.'

I put Mr Kent's leg back in the corner. It wasn't a whole leg — just the lower part of his right leg.

'I've been living without a leg since before you were born and I don't need your help now.'

Mr Kent had lost his leg in a motorbike accident when he was 25. He had never married, always lived alone and never had to depend on anybody for anything — well, apart from the prosthesis manufacturer.

I was just trying to help him strap the thing on — speed things up a bit because he was taking so long to get ready. I know it sounds terribly impatient of me, but he looked helpless as he groped for his walking stick while struggling to sit up in bed.

Once Mr Kent had his leg strapped on and was on his feet he was a different person. He was mobile and, if not exactly nimble, he could move pretty quickly.

'I don't need to be here, it will pass,' he kept saying.

And every time, I responded the same way: 'It's just a precaution, the doctors know what they're doing; you'll probably be home in no time at all.'

Mr Kent was a very strong willed man. He was so fiercely protective of his independence that he would not let any of the nurses help him in any way. The closest he had come to asking for assistance, was pointing his walking stick at the television and saying, 'Be a good lad will you and change the channel for me.'

But for all his tough demeanour, I suspected he was more worried than he let on.

Mr Kent had been admitted to hospital because he had woken up one morning and found that the left side of his mouth was not quite working properly. When he had gone to look in his bathroom mirror, he noticed that this side of his mouth was drooping slightly.

The hospital doctors were concerned that Mr Kent might have had a small stroke, or even just a TIA (a Transient Ischaemic Attack — a mini-stroke).

'A mini-stroke, now I've heard it all, next you'll be trying to admit me,' and of course they did.

Luckily none of Mr Kent's limbs appeared to have been affected: there was no telltale weakness or paralysis in his arms or legs; and even though his mouth had a slight droop, his swallowing had not been affected.

On the third morning of Mr Kent's stay with us the doctor decided to change his medicine slightly. For the last five years Mr Kent had been taking half an aspirin a day; the doctor now wanted to give him an enteric-coated aspirin, which has a protective outside layer so it's less rough on the stomach. It was a good idea of the doctor; Mr Kent should have been on this medication years ago.

Aspirin is one of the most common drugs given to patients, but it can help prevent some serious problems. It thins the blood, thus reducing the risk of clots forming, lessening the likelihood of strokes (clots in the brain) and heart attacks (clots in the arteries that supply the heart).

The only problem was Mr Kent seemed a touch reluctant to take the new enteric-coated aspirin.

'I've made it this far on my own with one leg and I will not be told what's good for me by a boy.'

I could feel my face turning red as I sensed the eyes of the three other patients in the room on me. I had no reason to be embarrassed, and I certainly needn't have felt stupid, but I did.

I suppose Mr Kent's stubbornness was a way for him to stay in control of the situation, but I was resolute: I would make him see reason and win, especially as I had an audience. After all, it was for his own good.

'If it makes you happier, I'll have the doctor come in and explain things again,' I offered, but Mr Kent just sat there with his arms crossed.

'I don't want to talk to him either,' Mr Kent said, referring to the junior doctor. 'I want to see someone old enough to know what they're doing.'

'Well, I can't force you to take it,' I said, changing tactics and making as if to exit the room.

'Hold on a minute,' Mr Kent piped up, 'I never said I wouldn't take the blasted thing.'

Why the sudden change of heart? Again, it was another way for Mr Kent to retain some control of his situation.

'Get the doc. I'll listen to what he has to say and then decide.'

I didn't argue. Soon the doctor reassured Mr Kent that the change was in his best interest. Fifteen minutes later, the battle was over and I was the victor — although it didn't really feel like a victory. As Mr Kent brought the aspirin to his lips he kept his eyes glued on mine; he wasn't smiling and he certainly wasn't happy. It wouldn't have surprised me if he gave in just to have some peace and quiet.

With a sense of relief I left Mr Kent to his own

devices and walked away down the corridor feeling at least content in the knowledge that I had done what was right, even if Mr Kent wasn't 100 per cent convinced . . .

Beeeeeeepbeeeeeeeeeeep!

It was coming from Mr Kent's room. Someone was probably sitting on their call bell — at least I hoped that was it — but as I turned around and hurried back to his room, I had a sinking feeling in my stomach.

I entered Mr Kent's room and his eyes locked on to mine. He was struggling to sit up and reach his walking stick, but the right side of his body didn't seem to be working very well. He kept on falling back on to his pillows. His right arm wasn't doing what he wanted; it seemed to be determined to lie there like a lump of lead. His droop had worsened and his mouth was hanging slightly open. Mr Kent was having a stroke right in front of me.

I watched, with mouth agape and a sickening feeling in my stomach. The stroke didn't stop him from being able to talk. 'You've done this to me; you've killed me.'

I'm sure his voice must have been slurred, but I heard every word very clearly.

My skin broke out in goosebumps. I tried to help Mr Kent sit up but he waved his good arm in my face.

'Get away. You've done enough damage already.'

I could feel the eyes of all the other patients in the room on me: disbelieving, shocked, accusing. I was to blame; it was my fault — I had forced him to take the new aspirin. At least, that was how they must all have seen this. I was responsible for setting this man on the path to death.

I couldn't think rationally. I tried to help Mr Kent again; this time he didn't speak to me, instead he made a loud moaning noise, a noise that spoke volumes. His stroke was progressing rapidly.

It felt like forever before the other nurses rushed in to find me standing there doing nothing — immobilised by shock; racked with guilt. The doctor was called and I left the room on the verge of tears. I was in no state to see any of my other patients. I knew if I went in to see one, I would no longer be able to hold back the flood.

Worst of all is that part of what Mr Kent said was true: the stroke probably was the end of him. Even if he survived, the effect the stroke would have on his mobility would be a huge blow, especially with a prosthetic leg. Once mobility is gone it's never good; it's a very slippery slope, especially in the aged.

Looking back now, I realise that Mr Kent's stroke had nothing to do with either me or with the new aspirin. However, in Mr Kent's mind, I was to blame. If he is still alive today, he probably still blames me, probably genuinely believes it was my fault. That is not a nice feeling, but I have come to understand that there are some things you cannot change and I can live with it.

I left work that day feeling as miserable as I

ever had felt in my life. I was still battling with tears. I was only 21 years old, and just like he had said only a short time ago, still a boy really.

The meaning of teamwork

Mr Simpson was 45, fit, and an avid golfer. His biggest worry was whether he would still be able to play after the surgery he was having the next day. I explained that if all went well in the operating theatre, there should be no reason why he couldn't continue to play golf.

Mr Simpson was by no means my first surgical patient, but he was the first patient that I had prepared for his type of operation. He was going to have a femoral popliteal bypass graft. Basically, the circulation to one of his legs was rubbish, and the surgeon was going to put in some new plumbing that would fix the problem. If the surgery wasn't performed, Mr Simpson could eventually lose the leg.

As horrendous as my recent experience with Mr Kent had been, I felt happier in my new environment. It certainly helped that I wasn't dealing exclusively with sensitive matters pertaining to female health, but the main reason things felt better was because of the team I was working with.

Katie was the nurse in charge for the shift, and she was great. Katie was always there to lend me a hand. Whenever I needed help with a wash, a lift, a wound dressing, advice of any kind, she was the person I turned to. Katie had already asked me several times if I was going to be okay looking after Mr Simpson on my own, and after reassuring her that I felt I could cope, she made it clear that I could come to her for help or advice, no matter how trivial. Knowing I had some support gave me a rare feeling of confidence.

Everything went smoothly and Mr Simpson was wheeled to the operating theatre at 7.30 in the morning. I didn't see him again until one o'clock that afternoon.

'How was it?' he asked me for the third time in the last hour. With leftover anaesthetic in his system and a pump infusing him with intermittent morphine, that sort of thing was to be expected. I reassured him all went well.

The next day Mr Simpson was a bit livelier, and asking about when he would be able to play golf, but I still would not give him a definite answer.

By the second day post-surgery, Mr Simpson was in fine spirits, mainly because there was live golf on the television. I left him in peace and reminded him to call if he needed anything.

Thirty minutes later Mr Simpson's bell went off.

'My leg feels worse; it's more painful than normal.'

Up until now his pain had been well controlled, so it was a bit of a surprise that it should start being a problem now.

I began to examine his leg, worried at what this could mean. I checked the pulses in his foot, to make sure the blood was still getting through. I examined his calf and his thigh. Thankfully there was no swelling. As a precaution I went to search for Katie and get her opinion.

I never got a chance to chat with Katie as I was distracted by the call bell of another of my patients.

Mr Dexter was one of my medical patients. He had pain in his chest, caused by angina. Simply put, the arteries supplying the heart were not letting enough blood through, resulting in poor oxygenation of the heart muscle. It's the lack of oxygen that causes the pain.

Mr Dexter had a small bottle of spray which he was supposed to squirt under his tongue whenever he had chest pain. The medicine dilated his blood vessels, including the ones that supply the heart. Hopefully this would allow more blood and, therefore, more oxygen to the heart muscle.

He explained that he had given himself a dose five minutes ago. I instructed him to give himself some more spray. It works very quickly, within moments of taking it. I waited the recommended five minutes to reassess.

'How bad is the pain now?'

I didn't get a chance to hear how the pain was, because the call bell in Mr Simpson's room went off, and continued to go off. It wasn't stopping. I ran to his room.

'Oh shit, it's agony,' Mr Simpson said as soon as he saw me.

I looked at his thigh and knee and placed my hands on them. I could feel something hard in his thigh. It wasn't swollen to the naked eye, but I could definitely feel a lump that wasn't there before. It was also hot. By the time I went to feel for a pulse in his foot, the other nurses on duty that shift were in the room.

Katie took charge, and within minutes had the doctor at the bedside. Katie told a terrified Mr Simpson that his graft wasn't working, and that he needed to go back to theatre.

The head surgeon was urgently called back into hospital. During the next hour, myself, the junior doctor and the registrar made what preparations we could to get him to theatre. That hour was probably the most terrifying in Mr Simpson's life. There was a chance that he would not only never play golf again, but possibly lose the leg altogether.

When he finally left for the operating room, the last of the adrenaline left my body and I felt physically and emotionally drained. It was also at that moment that I remembered Mr Dexter and his chest pain, as well as my other four patients that I hadn't seen in all that time. I ran to Mr Dexter's room, expecting to find him either clutching his chest in agony or dead.

He was sitting up reading his book. 'Are you okay?'

'Why shouldn't I be?' he replied.

I briefly felt relieved, but I rushed to check on my other four patients. Their medications were late . . .

. . . but they'd all had their meds. They were comfortable. All their needs had been taken care of.

Katie and the other nurses had seen to every one of my other patients.

This kind of generosity was not to be unique.

Over the next two years I learnt that, in this ward at least, it was normal; the nurses worked as a team, and always watched out for each other.

Big man, big heart

Part 1: Who is Mr Groom?

Feeling part of a team was what made nursing truly enjoyable for me. I no longer dreaded going to work each day. I didn't have that nauseous feeling in my stomach whenever I had to approach a senior member of staff. The biggest improvement was in the confidence I felt about looking after more challenging types of patients, which was fortunate because I was about to encounter one of my biggest challenges yet.

'Are you okay having Mr Groom again?' asked Carol, the nurse in charge.

What could I say? No, I'm worn out, he's too heavy, too much work?

I had been looking after Mr Groom for what felt like forever and was hoping for a bit of a break, but whenever it came time to allocate his nurse there was always a silence in the office.

My adventures with Mr Groom had begun four days ago. I had just returned from my days off. The problem with coming back from time off is that you are at the bottom of the priority list when it comes to picking and choosing patients. To be fair, everyone is generally pretty reasonable when allocating patients, everyone takes their share of the demanding ones, but every now and then there comes along one patient whom no one really wants to be responsible for.

The first time I had met Mr Groom, I couldn't believe my eyes; before me lay a sweating, rippling, heaving mass of flesh, covered almost head to toe in traditional Maori tattoos. He was one of the most obese men that I have ever had to look after. He must have been at least 180 kilograms.

Carol tried to be encouraging. 'He needs someone strong and you've done so much for him; you're good for him.'

I didn't see exactly how I was good for him. We were too different. I come from an average white family, from an average white part of town. Mr Groom is an ex-member of Black Power, a gang with offices throughout New Zealand. Not a group to cross — even an ex-member — they eat boys like me for lunch.

'Good morning, how are you?' I asked Mr Groom.

At the sound of my voice he rolled over towards me, the bed springs protesting beneath him, and greeted me with a huge, gap-toothed grin.

'Morning,' he replied, then, after pausing to catch his breath, 'Could be better, bro.'

Poor Mr Groom, he was only 35 years old, but he looked ten years older and had all the problems you would expect in someone twice his age. I could tell just from looking at his swollen legs, that it wasn't all fat — there was fluid in them, a sure sign of a failing heart. Just to prove myself right, I poked my index finger into his ankle and left an indentation that faded away very slowly. Mr Groom's joints also looked swollen and I wondered how much longer they would put up with being abused, before giving out completely.

Mr Groom had never been in hospital before, but he'd developed a bad case of pneumonia. In most 35-year-old men, a case of pneumonia would probably not need hospitalisation, but because of his weight he needed to be with us, especially now, because it looked like his condition was deteriorating.

With someone as big as Mr Groom, it's never really just a simple case of pneumonia. He already had a diagnosis of heart failure. His joints always ached, and it was an effort to walk, even when well.

Mr Groom was drenched in a cold sweat, his hands were shaking, and as I clasped his wrist, I could feel his pulse racing. His eyes had a glazed look about them, as if he was in a world of his own. But it was his laboured breathing that caused me most concern.

'How long has your breathing been this bad?' I asked him.

Surely he hadn't been struggling for breath all night? I knew the night staff would have done something.

'It just got bad in the last hour' — he paused to get his breath — 'started about six this morning' — pause — 'came on really quick.'

He smiled again at me.

'Why didn't you call the nurse sooner?'

A rather pointless question, it wasn't going to help, but I just had to know.

'They had a busy night' — pause — 'didn't want to bother them.'

Not the answer I was expecting.

There was no time to waste; I grabbed Carol who took one look at Mr Groom and immediately came to the same conclusion as I did. We went into the corridor to discuss our plan of action.

'We need to get Dr Grey down here right away,' Carol said.

'Are you sure?' I replied. 'Why don't we get the registrar instead?'

Dr Grey was the new junior doctor and had only qualified in the last few months. It's an unfortunate truth that some junior doctors don't listen to the nursing staff, and it looked like Dr Grey was turning into one of them. Just the other day we'd pointed out to him that one of his patients normally took his blood pressure medications in the evening before bed, because the patient said if he took them in the morning, he fainted. Dr Grey had disagreed and prescribed them for the morning, and sure enough the patient collapsed because of low blood pressure. The nurses were there to catch him. They also suggested perhaps reducing his dose, but this never happened either.

Carol thought over my suggestion for a moment or two.

'You may be right, but we've got to give Dr Grey a chance.'

Fortunately, today Dr Grey surprised us all.

He too took one look at our patient and did the wisest thing I had seen him do in three months. He called his registrar. Registrars usually have a minimum of four or five years of experience, and can usually be relied upon when complications arise.

The registrar took Mr Groom's pulse. It was weak, but pumping along at 110 beats per minute. His breathing was rapid and shallow; he also had a high fever. Mr Groom had developed a sepsis — meaning the infection had got into his bloodstream — and a sudden worsening of his heart failure on top of his pneumonia.

With these added complications, Mr Groom was in a very serious condition. The doctors contemplated transferring him to the intensive care unit, but due to a shortage of beds he stayed with us. He was so weak that he was unable to stand, or even sit himself up in bed; the most he could do was roll from side to side.

'It's pretty bad, isn't it?' Mr Groom asked me.

It was. He could potentially die, but all he did was smile at me. It seemed I was more worried than he was.

'Don't worry,' he said, 'I know you'll be able to fix me up.'

Was he trying to put me at ease, by putting on a brave front? If I were in his position I would be terrified. But his cool calm didn't seem to be an act. Did he, by some chance, have that much faith in us, a complete belief that the doctors and nurses will be able to do just that? I wish I had that much faith in myself.

Let the battle commence.

Part 2: Mission impossible

To give his medicines, Mr Groom had a tube stuck into the side of his neck and threaded towards the heart, because all the veins in his arms kept on collapsing.

He also had a tube put up his penis to accurately measure the fluids passing through his kidneys — especially important since his blood tests had shown that his kidneys were struggling. It was quite the balancing act, because too much fluid and his heart would struggle even more, while too little and his kidneys might deteriorate further.

Mr Groom had the girls from the physiotherapy department visiting twice a day, pounding on his chest, trying to help move the build-up of mucus in his lungs.

He had multiple blood tests alongside multiple antibiotics.

But for all the poking, prodding and discomfort that Mr Groom endured, he only had one small wish.

'I tell ya something, doc' — he'd developed the habit of calling me doc because I was male — 'get me in the shower and I will feel a new man. I can't take another bed sponge, mate.'

Imagine spending 24 hours in bed; I guarantee by the end of it you will be desperate for a shower. Mr Groom spent a total of 170 hours in bed.

The job of washing Mr Groom was a team event, with nearly all the staff involved. It took five people in total: three to roll him, one person to hold the bed still, because the brakes were not strong enough, and a fifth nurse to actually do the washing. But for all the sponge baths and changing of bed linen, I could never clean him as well as I wanted, or he wanted. It was understandable that Mr Groom's greatest wish was to have a shower, but he wasn't ready for a shower yet, he just wasn't well enough.

Thankfully, life slowly crept back into Mr Groom and it looked like we were going to win the fight. As his breathing settled down, his legs began to shrink, and he started asking when he would be able to get out of bed and joking about feeling like a beached whale. I laughed along with him, though it didn't feel quite right, because it was the response he was hoping for.

'Not long now, maybe tomorrow,' I always replied — never giving him an exact answer, but we were certainly beginning to make progress. I watched as Mr Groom went from bed to bedside, from there to reclining chair, from that to standing with a frame, then unassisted. It was at this stage that I decided he was well enough to have a shower.

★ ★ ★

'Um, I think it's a bit small,' said Mr Groom, looking down at the chair.

He was right, too. Even if we could have fitted him in the shower chair, I doubt it would have held his weight. I should have thought of this, and felt a touch stupid. I tried a normal wheelchair, but this was too small as well. I eventually managed to get hold of a chair used by the porters, which was half-again the size of an average wheelchair. These chairs are so big because they're used to take patients between various departments around the hospital, and the extra space is often used for things like oxygen bottles, notes and IV poles.

'Oh, that's pure fucking heaven,' were Mr Groom's first words as I turned the shower head on to him.

The water streaming off him was a dirty looking grey colour from the build-up of the sweat and dirt that I had never been able to completely get rid of.

'Harder. It won't hurt,' he told me as I scrubbed his back. 'I want it red and raw . . . Oh fuck that's good. I don't want another fucking bed sponge again, no offence intended, doc'

I wasn't offended, just pleased to see him happy. Mr Groom seemed to like having me around and I was discovering that I also enjoyed working with him, even though he was heavy work. I didn't see before me an intimidating ex-gang member, but a man in need of our help, a man who tried not to be a burden, a man now fighting for his life.

Any preconceptions I had had about Mr Groom had by now been turned on their head.

'Here, let me stand up and you can give my bum a good rub.'

He grabbed hold of the rail while I prepared to pull the chair away.

'On the count of three,' I said. 'Ready? One, two, three, heave.'

Something unexpected happened.

'Let's try again . . . and heave.'

I couldn't remove the chair.

He turned his head towards me; his face had an almost apologetic look.

'Guess I need to lose a few pounds.'

★ ★ ★

'What do you think?' I asked the nurses assembled in Mr Groom's room. 'All suggestions are welcome.'

I was greeted with silence and shrugged shoulders. Obviously, no one else had had this problem before, and as no one was coming up with a clever solution, I took the lead and tried the direct approach.

I positioned two nurses so they were holding Mr Groom's arms; another nurse and I held the chair steady, and the last nurse grabbed hold of the bed.

On the count of three everyone began heaving — biceps flexed; thighs braced.

'It's not going to work,' Carol grunted, as she pulled.

'It has to work,' I said through gritted teeth. 'Pull harder.'

Suddenly the chair released its victim and Mr Groom was catapulted on to his bed. The poor nurse whose job it had been to brace the bed was squashed as the bed crashed against the wall. The towels that were being used to cover Mr

Groom's nakedness landed on the floor, and there was a moment of shocked silence as everyone stared at the bare, quivering backside of Mr Groom as he lay straddled across the bed. I grabbed a towel off the floor and tried to cover him.

He began making a strange sound, his whole body convulsing. What had we done?

But I soon recognised the noise, and realised the convulsing wasn't a seizure, it was laughter. And not just a polite laugh to try to hide embarrassment, but a true, full-bodied, incapacitating, belly laugh; the contagious type.

Part 3: Missing parts

Mr Groom's sense of humour saved us all from feeling like absolute crap. In my short time as a nurse, I felt that nothing could top it.

Enter Dr Grey.

Dr Grey decided that as Mr Groom was getting better, it was time to have his urinary catheter removed.

'Surely not yet, doc, he's only just managed to stand on his own. Shouldn't we leave it at least another couple of days?' I asked.

'Absolutely not, it's been in there far longer than necessary, he's at risk of infection.'

The catheter is the plastic tube I mentioned earlier; it goes up the penis and straight into the bladder. It is an infection risk, as bugs can creep up it, but sometimes you have to weigh up the benefits against the risks. In Mr Groom's case, the risk was of him being incontinent in bed as he might not get a urine bottle in place in time. Urine is very good at breaking down skin, and Mr Groom did not need sores around his inner thighs, buttocks or scrotum. I tried to make this case.

I wasn't alone in thinking that it should be left in; all the nursing staff agreed. But the doctor didn't even budge when the charge nurse stepped in, and so the catheter was taken out.

The next day Mr Groom began to have some problems.

As predicted, he was not managing with a urine bottle.

Even after the previous day's shower, the smell coming from Mr Groom's lower regions was getting bad again.

Michelle was the nurse assigned to Mr Groom this shift, so it was up to her to deal with Dr Grey, but I was by her side when she confronted him.

'Can we put another catheter in?' Michelle asked. The doctor hesitated a moment, then looked at me, almost for confirmation. I nodded my head, and Dr Grey consented.

Of course, Dr Grey was not going to replace the catheter, because that was the nurse's job, and so that fell upon my friend Michelle.

I have known Michelle from my training days; she is a pretty blonde with a ready smile, a quick wit and a habit of over-dramatising things. Off she went with catheter in hand and the faithful rubber gloves. She came back from Mr Groom's room 15 minutes later.

56

'Can you lend a hand?' she asked me, a blush touching her cheeks. 'I'm having a bit of trouble.'

Trouble? There shouldn't be any trouble; he'd already had a catheter so there shouldn't be any obstruction.

'Sure, but what sort of trouble are you having?' I replied.

'I can't find it,' she told me.

'Find what exactly? The right equipment or the right size catheter?'

Michelle's face went red.

'No . . . I can't find his penis.'

With this statement, Michelle began to giggle. I walked back with her to Mr Groom's room to see if I could sort things out.

'What's the matter, doc?' Mr Groom asked me as I walked in the room.

Mr Groom couldn't see what was going on because he was lying almost flat and his stomach was in the way.

I didn't know what to say. I couldn't tell him that Michelle was unable to find his penis.

'Nothing's wrong,' I lied. 'Michelle just needs an extra pair of hands.'

I quickly put on some gloves and got down to business.

The penis wasn't there — there was absolutely no sign of it. Mr Groom was so overweight his penis seemed to have been sucked up into his belly. There wasn't even any sign of a scrotum. I glanced at Michelle who was redder than a beetroot and refusing to make eye contact with either me or the patient.

'Can you try pushing a bit over here?' I instructed Michelle, as we tried to coerce the thing out, by pushing on his bladder while I dug my fingers into the crevice where his penis should be.

'Hold this bit for me,' I instructed Michelle, as she used one hand to hold back his stomach.

No matter how hard we tried we couldn't find the penis.

'What's the problem, doc?' Mr Groom asked me again.

He didn't sound worried, just curious. It's just as well he couldn't see past the roundness of his belly because he couldn't see either my or Michelle's face. Michelle looked like she was having a spasm — her shoulders were shaking from trying to repress a dose of the giggles. I felt like slapping her, not just because it was so inappropriate, but because it was infectious. Nothing in my training had prepared me for this. But I was not going to let Michelle contaminate me.

I had to answer Mr Groom, but my mind struggled to come up with an answer that would not take away any last remaining shreds of dignity that we had not already stripped. I finally settled on a reply.

'How do you usually pee?' I asked as casually as I could.

'I just feel around for it a bit,' Mr Groom said, 'but I can't find it lying down, and when I need to pee, I can't stand up quickly enough.'

It all sounded very reasonable but his answer made me think.

'When you say you feel around for it, does that mean that you don't actually see your penis?'

There, I've just humiliated the man completely, but it might make our job easier if I know what we're up against.

'Haven't seen it in a few years,' he admitted, then fell silent.

Not wanting to admit defeat I went in again, while Michelle pushed down on his bladder with one hand while holding up his stomach with the other.

The conversation and situation were too much for Michelle and she began to cough, a cough which sounded suspiciously like a chuckle to me. She raced from the room, saying she had to go to the bathroom urgently. I told Mr Groom I was going to get the doctor and walked into the office to find Michelle red faced and worried. 'Do you think he noticed?' Michelle asked me. I could see Michelle was feeling guilty for not being able to keep away the giggles, so I reassured her she'd done the right thing by leaving the room, and that I was sure he hadn't noticed.

Eventually, we called the doctor and between the three of us we managed to find his penis and insert the catheter. The doctor was subdued and to his credit looked guilty while Michelle and I were just relieved we could keep a straight face.

Mr Groom was eventually discharged home; he weighed 30 kilograms less and felt like a new man.

'You've done good for me, doc, and don't be too hard on yourself, it was pretty fucking funny.'

Beware of toilet

One of the challenges of nursing is that you are constantly encountering new things. As a young nurse in my first year of work, *everything* was new. But there is one particular first experience that I will never forget.

Mr Smith was 82 years old. If he could have had it his way, he'd still have been living independently in his three-bedroom house with his quarter acre of land. His children and grandchildren, however, had convinced him that the best and safest option was for him to move into a small apartment that was part of a rest home — a nice balance between independence and supervision. But, after forgetting to turn off his stove several times in two weeks, Mr Smith's meals were now cooked for him, and after a fall getting out of the shower, he had an aide who helped him with his bathing. Still, other than that, Mr Smith looked after himself, which is pretty independent for an 82-year-old man.

Mr Smith was brought into the ward at eight o'clock on a Sunday evening. His chest was heaving as he strained to pull air into his lungs; you could hear him wheezing, coughing and spluttering from outside his room. Mr Smith had been a bit off-colour for nearly a week. What had started out as a mild cough had gradually stained his handkerchief with white, then yellow, then green and now red speckled sputum. The infection had crept insidiously into his lungs, spreading lower and lower like a cancer. The nurses from the rest home had advised him to come to hospital earlier, but like many men in his position, he was stubborn and refused to move. By the time he agreed to go to hospital, he didn't really have a choice: it was go to hospital, or die.

I liked Mr Smith instantly.

'I'm only being a burden; just put me out of my misery,' he said between gasps.

He even managed a brief smile. It says a lot about a person's character when they can joke at a time like this.

I told him to stop talking rubbish; that once the medicines kicked in he would be feeling much better.

Forty-eight hours of intravenous antibiotics later, and Mr Smith was rapidly improving. He could speak whole sentences without getting out of breath. He was not coughing up so much sputum. He even managed to get himself up out of bed and into the reclining chair.

Watching your patient get better, knowing that you are one of the people responsible for making the difference, is one of the greatest feelings in the world — Though, while I'd love to be the one to take the credit for his progress, it's always a team effort. It wasn't only a matter of antibiotics fighting an infection: nurses cleaned, dressed, toileted, exercised and talked to the patient; the physiotherapist came in twice a day to exercise his chest; the laboratory and X-ray people visited daily to draw his blood and irradiate him.

Between us all, I was sure we would get Mr Smith back home.

It was Wednesday, Mr Smith's fourth night in hospital, and he and I were discussing the merits of a commode versus a regular toilet.

Like most patients, Mr Smith had never liked using the commode, but up until now he had been too sick to risk walking too far from the bed. 'I won't sit on that disgusting thing again. There are other people in here and it is embarrassing.'

He had a point: there's no way to completely hide the smells and sounds that go with taking a dump in a shared room.

'I'm not using it and that is final.' Mr Smith was adamant, and began to get out of bed. 'You could try making yourself useful by handing me my walking stick.'

I had a vision of Mr Smith collapsing in the middle of the corridor: 'Please, wait a moment and I'll grab you a wheelchair.'

To make things easier, I used a portable shower chair, so that once I had him seated I could just roll it straight over the toilet and he wouldn't have to move one bit. As I wheeled him down the corridor I noticed he was still wheezing, not nearly as badly as he had been on admission, but I still set him up with some portable oxygen to help things out.

Naturally, I wasn't keen to leave Mr Smith alone, so I waited discreetly outside the partially open bathroom door, calling out every 30 seconds, 'Are you okay in there?'

To which he responded, 'Can't a man take a crap in peace?'

But on my fourth call, Mr Smith was silent, and then I heard a thump. My heart leapt into my throat as I rushed in.

Mr Smith was still sitting in the chair, but he had slumped against the wall with his eyes staring sightlessly ahead. His nose and lips were a bluish purple, and darkening before my eyes.

This was it: my first arrest.

I'd actually felt a little envious of fellow student nurses who had been involved in an arrest during their training. I'd also heard experienced nurses casually talking over lunch break, 'Oh yeah, Mr Brown, he was in VF and we shocked him a number of times; we got lucky — he pulled through.'

But this wasn't exciting like I'd imagined. I couldn't ever envisage casually discussing this over a sandwich. This was a nice old man whom I liked and who seemed to like me. A man who had been getting better.

An arrest can refer to arrested breathing, or an arrested heart. In Mr Smith's case, he definitely wasn't breathing, and if his heart hadn't already stopped, it would very soon.

I called out for help, shouting down the corridor, and kept my finger on the call bell, until the doctor and another nurse came running.

The bathroom is not the easiest place to begin

CPR and neither is a shower chair.

'Grab his shoulders and don't let him fall,' Dr Jackson instructed as we wheeled him back to his room.

Between the three of us we literally threw him on to his bed and the doctor barked at me to push the arrest alarm.

The alarm was in the corridor. I walked past it dozens of times each day — in fact, I'd often wondered if I would ever get to push it — but suddenly it had disappeared. It should have been right in front of me, but the wall seemed so damned big at that moment.

It could have only been about ten seconds before I found it, but each of those seconds was one more in which the life was draining out of my patient. I jammed my finger on the button — which, of course, had been in front of me the whole time — and raced back into the room.

The doctor yelled at me to begin compressions. Holy shit, compressions. I jumped on Mr Smith's chest and began pumping up and down at a furious rate, while the other nurse used an Ambubag to pump air into his lungs. The doctor was trying to get some intravenous access, because Mr Smith's bid line wasn't working — what a horrendous time for a line to pack up. I hoped they wouldn't blame me for that; he was my patient after all. I could see the swelling around the old IV site where the doctor had tried to inject some medicine.

'Not so hard,' the other nurse said to me, as I

felt a sickening crunch as a rib or two cracked under my hands.

Within a minute, the arrest team arrived and the professionals took over. They asked me to stand back while they did their work, and in my hurry to get out of their way I knocked over the drinks bottle that was sitting on the bedside. It's a strange thing to remember at a time like this, but it was a glass bottle full of blackcurrant concentrate, and when it hit the floor it splattered bright red everywhere, like fresh arterial blood.

As the arrest team got underway, I was amazed at how calm, quiet and confident they all were whereas I was shaking from all the adrenaline pumping through me. I watched as they hooked Mr Smith up to a monitor and wondered if they were going to shock him with the defibrillator, but it was too late for that. He had no electrical activity left in his heart.

In a lot of TV shows, someone yells 'Stand clear', and they shock the patient with some paddles, but Mr Smith didn't need this. In fact, most TV shows get it wrong. Those shocks don't start the heart, they actually stop the heart. When a heart arrests, the electrical activity which once made the heart beat doesn't stop immediately: it goes haywire, shooting in all directions. It makes the heart a quivering jelly, shaking with all that uncontrolled current. When we shock someone, we're trying to briefly stop this craziness, in the hope that the patient's own heart will start again in a healthy rhythm. Another way to think of it is a lifeguard who swims out to rescue a drowning swimmer, but the swimmer is so panicked, the rescuer can't do his job, so the rescuer slaps them really hard, to shock them into calming down.

Sadly, Mr Smith died that night and it was not a nice way to die; he was sitting on the toilet for goodness' sake. The nurse with me during the arrest was Rose. She was in her early fifties, and had been a nurse all her life. She could see how shaken I was and took me aside for a quiet word.

'There's nothing you could have done,' Rose said to me, 'it's quite common for people to die on the toilet.'

Registering my surprise Rose told me that it's not unusual for people to want to empty their bowels before having a heart attack. She then explained that the effort to try to pass a bowel motion was often the trigger that set it off. She even said she'd lost a few in the toilet over the years.

But, instead of feeling better, I began to feel guilty. I shouldn't have let him go. I knew he should have stayed in his room and used the commode.

'It's not your fault,' Rose repeated, then let out a brief chuckle. 'There's no use feeling guilty. When it's your time, there's nothing we can do.'

Rose's words helped a bit but there was still a sense of guilt. I was determined never to let any of my elderly patients use the toilet again; they could wait for the next shift to come on.

Rose offered to help me prepare Mr Smith for his family, who would arrive shortly. This was another new experience for me.

As we began to wash Mr Smith, Rose did something unexpected. Every time she did something to Mr Smith's body, she would use his name and explain what she was doing, just as you would with a living patient. She was gentle, and spoke softly. You could tell she still cared.

Heartless

'I've learnt my lesson,' Mr Holdsworth said, pausing to look me in the eye for emphasis, before continuing. 'I've learnt it the hard way.'

I nodded my head in sympathy, even though I'd heard the story at least three times. He seemed to think of himself as some self-sacrificing guru of wisdom; wisdom gained through pain and suffering. Well, I guess he was at least part right.

'Don't make the same mistakes I ... arrrgh — ' He never finished his sentence because he was clutching his chest.

Having looked after Mr Holdsworth during his last two admissions, I was quite used to his frequent attacks of chest pain.

I placed an oxygen mask on Mr Holdsworth's face, told him I'd be back shortly, and left the room. When I returned I was armed with morphine. 'This should do the trick,' I said as I injected the narcotic directly into his vein.

Often providing oxygen can be enough to relieve a patient's angina, but if this isn't enough, then morphine is another option. It not only relieves pain, but helps reduce the workload of the heart.

I watched Mr Holdsworth's expression as the pain slowly eased from his chest and an almost calm, albeit glazed, look came over his face. It's sometimes hard to believe that medicine can have such an amazing effect.

'How much that time?' Mr Holdsworth asked.

He always asked this and every time I was reluctant to answer. It's not as if he didn't need the medicine. People rarely ask how much. Maybe it was his background that made me reluctant, or maybe it was because I was giving him more each time, which meant his heart was getting worse.

'Thirty milligrams,' I reluctantly replied, avoiding his gaze.

'Hell, I've never had that much in one go.'

Mr Holdsworth didn't sound upset, more intrigued, as if curious about how much his body could take. You see, Mr Holdsworth used to be an intravenous drug user. Over the years that he had injected morphine into his veins, he had built up a resistance to the drug. This was also how he damaged his heart. Most of the damage occurred on the occasions he took so much that his breathing stopped (one of the primary risks of morphine). Once his breathing stopped, it wasn't long before his heart stopped. Fortunately paramedics were able to revive him. Each time, he survived, but the damage to his heart was permanent.

'Not a good sign is it?' he added.

Sometimes it pays to tell the truth, even when it can hurt, but it's still hard. Should I tell him that I've never given such a high dose of morphine in one push, or given it as frequently to one patient, in my entire career? Should I tell him that I'm even a little nervous giving 20 to 30 milligrams pushes of morphine every half an

69

hour? He probably already knows this, especially given his background. He probably already knows that for most people one to two milligrams is a sufficient amount.

'You're probably just having a bad day,' I replied with false bravado and an equally false smile.

'Now I know you're trying to be nice, but stop the bullshit. You know as well as I that I probably won't make it to Christmas.'

Mr Holdsworth tried to say this as casually as if he was talking about the weather, but I could tell his efforts were as forced as mine.

'You're still young, there is a chance. Something could happen any day.'

Unfortunately, Mr Holdsworth had had his first heart attack at the relatively young age of 36. It had been his first wake-up call, but now after four heart attacks, and four subsequent areas of dead, scarred heart muscle, there was very little that either drugs or a healthy lifestyle could do to help him. Christmas was one month away and unless a miracle happened Mr Holdsworth was probably not going to see it.

Still, we had to hope, sometimes it's all that keeps us going, and there was *one* chance, one possibility, that we could help Mr Holdsworth. At the age of 47, the only thing that could save him was a new heart, but after five years on the waiting list already, it seemed a very small chance indeed.

With Mr Holdsworth's rapidly declining health, the topic of conversation was often how much longer he would last, and whether a miracle would happen.

'I feel sorry for him . . . sometimes,' Jenny said to all the other nurses in the office, 'but at other times, I think he doesn't deserve our compassion, or a new heart.'

'I know we're supposed to be caring, but we're only human,' I said to Jenny. 'Today I felt sorry for the poor guy, but I'm like you. I don't always have much sympathy for him.'

As I looked around at the other nurses in the office I could tell, by the nodding heads, that we all seemed to have similarly mixed feelings. 'I guess it doesn't really matter what we think now,' Jenny continued, 'he's paying for his mistakes.'

Four weeks passed. It was now only a few days until Christmas Day. The girls had been busy decorating the ward, and I nearly broke my neck balancing precariously on a patient's bedside cabinet to put the finishing touches to the tree. I love this time of year — everyone is in such great spirits — even the patients don't seem so sick.

With half the ward empty we had time to sit around gossiping and reminiscing about who was the drunkest at the Christmas party — until it came time for me to check on Mr Holdsworth.

'How much that time?' he asked.

'Forty milligrams,' I replied. 'Is it enough?' I added.

He had stopped clutching his chest but his face was still creased with pain.

'Could you try a little more, just another ten? That should do the trick.'

The instructions given to us by the consultant were to give Mr Holdsworth whatever it took to

71

keep him comfortable, so I administered a further ten. With the additional dosage the last vestiges of pain left his face.

'You've been good to an old fool like me,' Mr Holdsworth said.

'We all make mistakes,' I replied.

'It won't be long now and I'll pay the ultimate price.'

My mind was blank. There was no suitable response. I chose that moment to leave the room, my Christmas spirit well and truly dampened.

The next morning something strange happened; as I headed towards the nurses' station I found myself taking a detour until I was standing outside Mr Holdsworth's room. The first thing I noticed was that his name had been removed from the door; the second was the deathly silence in the room.

I felt strangely depleted. I think that deep down, I had been believing that a Christmas miracle might happen. I quietly opened the door and there, staring me in the face, was an empty room. I headed to the office, where the nurses seemed to have gone mad.

Jenny greeted me with a big smile. 'Have you heard the news?'

I didn't know what news she was thinking. I know we all had mixed feelings about Mr Holdsworth, but it didn't seem quite right to be so damn happy first thing in the morning when a patient has just passed away.

'It's Mr Holdsworth,' she was almost exuberant. 'They came for him last night. They found a donor. He's getting a new heart.'

Everyone in the office was so genuinely happy that he was going to have a chance at life — regardless of whatever past mistakes he had made. Without a doubt that had to be the best Christmas present ever.

Mr Holdsworth's transplant operation had taken place far away in a big city hospital, so Jenny had to phone the hospital every few days to get an update on how our patient was doing.

'He could be discharged soon,' Jenny informed us, three weeks after he had been taken away. 'The doctors say he is doing really well. No sign of rejection.'

Three months later and Mr Holdsworth was back at home and living a normal life — although, we assumed, a much more careful, healthy life. It makes sense that a near death experience makes a person wiser.

During the two and a half years I had spent with patients in the medical/surgical ward, I thought I'd seen it all. I had seen how high the human spirit can soar, and then how low and selfish humanity can be. But then, along would come someone new, who would set up new boundaries, whether high or low.

One April morning I was greeted by Jenny, who had news to share: 'Mr Holdsworth is in the emergency room.'

'Organ rejection,' I blurted out.

'Oh no, it's much worse than that' — *What could be worse than your body rejecting your new heart?* — 'He's back to his old habits. He's overdosed on morphine.'

Jenny didn't attempt to hide the scorn in her voice.

'But that's not even the worst part. When he gets out of here, he's got an interview with the police. It seems he's been selling it as well.'

I guess not everyone learns from their mistakes. As I look back at some of the ambivalent feelings I had had while looking after Mr Holdsworth, I wonder if deep down I doubted that he really had changed. That heart could have gone to someone else less likely to waste it. I try not to judge, but the fact is we're all human and we do have opinions. I just hope that as a nurse, I can always accept people for who they are and give them the best care that I can.

Making a difference

'Mr Henderson has taken a turn for the worse,' Colleen read to the assembled nurses. 'He wouldn't get out of bed today and his chest is sounding bad.'

Colleen looked pretty upset about this; moisture was pooling in the corners of her eyes. Colleen was straight out of training and hadn't lost a patient yet; everyone was wondering if Mr Henderson was going to be her first.

All of the nurses liked Mr Henderson; he was a truly genuine, down-to-earth sort of man, with a heart of gold. At the age of 69 he should still have had some good years in front of him, but he had a bad case of pneumonia that the antibiotics couldn't seem to get rid of.

'The doc requested another chest X-ray. The infection hasn't improved at all,' she continued. 'He even thought it was a bit worse. Every breath Mr Henderson takes is an effort. It's horrible to listen to.'

The sound of a rattling, bubbling, straining set of lungs is never nice.

Everyone kept quiet — we had all had our first lost patient, and though Colleen might shed a few tears if Mr Henderson passed away, she would eventually recover.

With the report over, we filed quietly out of the office, talking with muted voices about the patient, as if he had already passed.

I was helping Colleen with Mr Henderson that day. As I entered his room, I took in his sickly grey skin. 'Good afternoon, Mr Henderson, I hear you've been giving the girls a bit of trouble.'

This brought a smile to his face. 'Could be better, son,' he rasped.

That was Mr Henderson, having a joke in the face of death. I grabbed a passing nurse and together we heaved him upright in his bed to help his breathing.

'I don't think I have much time,' Mr Henderson said to me when his coughing passed. 'I've had a good life. I'm not ashamed of the life I've led.'

I felt a lump in my throat.

'It's not over yet, Mr Henderson' — I had to at least *try* to be optimistic — 'The doc has just started you on a new antibiotic; you might feel like a new man tomorrow. Besides, you can't go letting young Colleen down after all her hard work.'

Mr Henderson managed a wry chuckle before bursting into another round of coughing.

'You're a bad liar, but you and the wee lass have done a lot for me — it would be a shame to disappoint you.'

Still, I wished there was something more I could do. Often it's just a case of being there for a patient, and willing to listen. Every so often, though, there's the option of doing something extra. Later that evening I had a chat with the other nurses about how we could make Mr Henderson more comfortable.

'Room 5 is free. What do you say to that?' I asked Rose.

'The poor fella is in a four-bedded room. It's not nice for him, or for the others in the room. Let's move him,' Colleen added.

This was the same Rose who'd been with me during my first patient death. She was the acting charge nurse for the late shift. She had as much experience as most of us on the ward put together, but she would never be a full-time ward manager. For her, nursing was a hands-on profession. Hands on patients, not hands on pen and paper. Once you started to move up the nursing ranks to managing you lost a lot of that daily contact with your patients. Thankfully, Rose approved the move.

What's so great about room number 5? Just ask Mr Henderson.

'I never get bored with the view,' he told Colleen and I as we gave him his bed sponge.

It was early summer and the view from his window was pretty spectacular. It was on the top floor, and looked out over the local gardens and playground. From room 5 you could see mums and dads playing with their children; you could watch as young couples strolled through the rose garden; and, best of all, room 5 was at the end of the ward and had windows on both sides, so it was possible to watch both the sun rise and the sun set.

'It sure is lovely,' Colleen said. 'I don't think I would get bored either.'

Still, Mr Henderson had been in room 5 for over a week now, but had only slightly improved.

'I guess it must be frustrating to be so close, yet so far,' I added.

I don't often make such shrewd observations, but I just knew that Mr Henderson would give anything to be outside in the fresh air. He didn't reply, though; he had dozed off to sleep, but little did I know how much my comment had affected Colleen.

★ ★ ★

It was a gorgeous, early summer Sunday afternoon and now Mr Henderson's fourth week in hospital. Unfortunately, he had taken another slight turn for the worse. It's not uncommon for a patient's health to have its ups and downs. The infection in his lungs had spread throughout his body. The doctors were using terms like sepsis and triple antibiotic therapy, but nothing we administered seemed to make any difference.

Colleen, however, had an idea that she felt sure would.

'Come on guys, what harm can it do? We're not exactly busy — we have the time.'

All the nurses in the office shook their heads. Colleen's idea was to take Mr Henderson, bed and all, out into the garden. It was a hell of a risk to take. If anything happened while he was out there, out of the controlled environment of the ward, we could lose our jobs. If his breathing got worse suddenly, or he had a heart attack, he could die.

'Look guys, you all think he's going to die anyway, so why not do this? Who's going to complain if something happens? He doesn't have any family, at least none that have bothered to visit him. Imagine if it was your father or grandfather lying there.'

That clinched it — five minutes later we all gave the plan the go-ahead. We even managed to coerce the junior doctor on duty into keeping his mouth shut.

There were four of us in total: two porters to push the bed, one nurse to push the emergency equipment and one for good luck. 'Don't stop breathing on us, Mr Henderson, at least not until we get back,' I said as we wheeled him along the corridor.

'I'll try my best,' Mr Henderson replied.

It was the most upbeat I had seen him in over a week.

We wheeled Mr Henderson out of a side door, along a foot-path and into the gardens. Unsurprisingly, people stopped and stared.

Others came over to say hello.

One boy came and asked, 'What's wrong, mister?' and Mr Henderson responded with the happiest look — a look that I've not forgotten.

★　★　★

I don't know if it was the feeling of wind on his face, the sensation of breathing in fresh summer air, the smell of the freshly cut grass and roses, or even the sound of children playing, but Mr Henderson came alive.

'Mr Henderson's white cell count has gone down and this morning's chest X-ray shows less infection,' said the junior doctor to his consultant. White cells in our blood fight infection — as a general rule, the higher their count, the worse the infection. The consultant just nodded his head as if he expected this, and why shouldn't he? After all, Mr Henderson was receiving the best care that modern medicine had to offer.

Not only were Mr Henderson's blood tests and X-rays looking better, but he was looking better himself. The grey pallor had left his skin. His breathing was also less strained. Somehow experiencing the outside world had made a huge difference, where medicine had failed. Perhaps by being so close to all that life and energy, some of it seeped in.

It was amazing to watch Mr Henderson progress: moving from lying in bed, to sitting on the edge of his bed. Before long he was taking his first few tentative steps, soon upgrading from walking with a frame and two nurses to one nurse and a walking stick.

He took his walking stick with him on the day of his discharge.

While the team of doctors quietly congratulated themselves on a job well done, we knew that it was Colleen who had made the difference. She had taken a risk, one that could have turned out very differently. Though, when I look back now, I don't think Mr Henderson would ever have let us down. He would have stayed alive just to keep us out of trouble.

Helpless, but that's okay

Sometimes it's possible to have the best of intentions, but get things wrong; in some cases, there is a very fine balance between doing just enough to help a patient, and doing too much.

It was particularly hard seeing Mr Belford in hospital — he was such a physical, athletic sort of man, even in his eighties. You could tell he had spent a lifetime working outdoors — his body was lean, hard and tanned. He had never smoked and never been much of a drinker. But even being such a fine physical specimen, I still thought he was far too old to have been standing on the back of a truck, unloading cattle.

Mr Belford was with us after one of the cows had become restless and had knocked him from the back of the truck, causing him to hit his head on the ground very hard. The knock had been so severe he had developed symptoms akin to having a stroke.

'I'll get them to move,' Mr Belford said, as he struggled to wiggle the fingers on his left arm.

Only 24 hours since his accident and the fingers were already looking like a set of claws.

'I hope so,' I replied — there are no certainties when dealing with head injuries.

Mr Belford had difficulty moving his left leg as well, but thankfully his speech was okay and although he was unsteady on his feet, he was still able to walk with a stick. Mr Belford lived alone, had never married, and had always done everything for himself. Aged bachelors like Mr Belford are generally pretty strong willed, even argumentative.

'I'm not helpless,' he said to me one morning, as I laid out his breakfast tray for him.

I had arranged extra-large eating utensils and made sure everything on the tray was in easy reach of his good hand.

'Just doing my job,' I replied, trying to make light of his comment.

'That may be,' he grumbled, 'but there are more sick than me in this place. Go take care of someone who needs some caring. I can take care of myself.'

Having by then had numerous dealings with stroke patients, I wasn't upset by Mr Belford's words. I had learnt that anger is a natural reaction.

I left Mr Belford in peace — but not without making sure he had his call bell within easy reach.

I felt I knew all there was to know about dealing with Mr Belford's situation. I was about to learn a simple, but important lesson.

★   ★   ★

'Did you see that?'

It was Mr Belford's ninth day with us, and small miracles had begun to happen.

'I saw it,' I replied, as I watched him slowly move his fingers.

The movement wasn't perfect, it was awkward

and uncontrolled, but it was a great sign. His walk had also become steadier, although he would always be left with a slight limp and in need of a walking stick. He would never be able to climb on trucks or herd cattle again. Despite all the progress, things were going to be different now in Mr Belford's life; he could never be completely independent again.

'Can I help you with that?' I asked, as he began to button up his shirt.

His affected fingers weren't nimble enough, so he was struggling with his good hand.

'I'm okay,' he replied.

'Are you sure?' I asked again.

He was really struggling. I watched as it took him two minutes to do up one button.

'Here, let me,' I said, as I quickly stepped in.

'Get ya hands off me,' Mr Belford bellowed at me, as if I was one of his farm dogs.

I leapt back, stammering an apology, 'I only wanted to help.'

Mr Belford stared at me in silence for a moment. The angry expression on his face began to fade.

'I know you mean well, lad,' he said.

Embarrassed, I felt my face redden.

'But my life is different now. I can't do the big things I used to do only a couple of weeks ago.'

His voice was hoarse. He'd always shown the tough, weathered old man-of-the-land exterior. This was a new side.

'But the small things mean a lot now — like making it to the toilet on time, doing up my shirt, cooking my own dinner. It may take for-bloody-ever, but it's important.'

Mr Belford was eventually sent to the rehabilitation unit, where he spent another three weeks. In that time, not only did he continue to do well physically, but everything was put in place to make sure that when he went home, he would be as independent as possible. Things like handrails being installed in the toilet and shower. A cleaner was arranged to help once a week, as well as a district nurse who would also be visiting him weekly. He was assessed to make sure he could cook his meals, and his neighbours were made aware of his situation and they promised to keep a close eye on him.

Thanks to Mr Belford, I started to think twice before rushing in to help right away. I learnt to be patient, and realised that the little things can mean a lot to a person, and make a big difference.

Golden years

During my time in Ward 13, the number of men I saw with prostate problems was extraordinary; it was almost as if they were an accepted part of ageing. Almost all of our urology patients were men needing some form of prostate treatment. (There were exceptions: the occasional female patient, who certainly wasn't there to have their prostate checked — although it wouldn't have surprised me to find someone looking for it.)

Some things get better with age; other things can only be appreciated with age. I am quite a long way from my golden years, but the more I dealt with the elderly, the more I found myself wondering if I would eventually suffer some of the ills that often come with growing old — and *when*. I started questioning whether my own water flow was as strong as it used to be. I'd never previously worried about how far I could pee or how easily I could make the colourful blocks of deodorant sitting in the bottom of the urinal move.

And, if I was worrying then, imagine how the patients with actual diagnosed prostate problems felt.

★   ★   ★

Mr Riley was desperate when he was brought into the ward. He had never had a problem with his waterworks before, although he had noticed that he was peeing smaller and more frequent amounts lately. He thought he could solve the problem by drinking more — and that is just what he did; he drank litre after litre of water. So, it was a bad time for his urethra to block off completely.

When we met him, Mr Riley was writhing on the bed in agony.

'Please do something — please oh please — the pain is unbearable,' he pleaded.

His looked to be a simple problem, hopefully easily fixed, so I didn't waste any time getting Dr King, the junior doctor, to see him.

I didn't want to palpate the bladder, especially as I could see it protruding up from his lower abdomen, so I left that part to the doctor . . .

'What the hell was that for!? I could've told you it's full.'

Mr Riley nearly went through the roof as Dr King gently pushed on his lower abdomen. It wasn't really Dr King's fault — he was just doing what he had been trained to do: a complete and thorough assessment. He was a bit shaken, but he was new and probably hadn't seen someone in this much pain from a blocked urethra before.

'Perhaps we could catheterise him now,' I suggested.

The doctor readily agreed and we got started. I don't have words to describe the look of relief that swept over Mr Riley's features as the catheter was inserted and the pressure finally released — but I'll try anyway. Imagine spending a night out on the town drinking and waking up in the morning in urgent need of a pee. Now imagine that no matter how hard you tried, you could not pass a drop. Every minute, every hour the pressure keeps on building, the sensors in your bladder overloading with pressure, they're screaming out at you to do something, but there is nothing you can do. Then suddenly . . .

'I can't believe it. It's no wonder I was in agony,' Mr Riley said, as two litres of urine drained from his bladder.

You might think it impossible for a bladder to hold two litres of fluid, but what happens in cases like Mr Riley's is that over time the bladder slowly stretches . . . and stretches. It took ten minutes to completely empty.

Mr Riley was now on the prostate surgery list; he was entering his prostatic golden years.

Unfortunately, the waiting list for urological surgery is often long and there are many older men sitting at home with a tube of their own because their plumbing has blocked up. Some of these men have spent longer than twelve months like this. Mr Riley didn't have private insurance and he now had to adapt to this new stage of his life.

It is unfortunate that we often have patients coming in to hospital because they have acquired an infection that has crept up this tubing and into their bladder, or patients whose catheters had blocked up because their urine was full of foul smelling lumps of dead tissue and bacteria. It seemed to me that more time and money was spent in the long run from these complications. And if anyone is going to get a complication it is most likely to be the elderly.

The veteran

Tom, Simon, Daryl and Joe were four patients who put a lot of trust in their urologist. At 75, Tom was the oldest of the men. He was a prostate veteran; this was going to be his second operation in three years. The rest of the men were virgins — all in their sixties and about to have a trim.

Being four men in the same room, all about to have the same operation, enabled the men to share notes and generally have a laugh (albeit a nervous one) at the situation.

'You gotta drink lots of water, that's the secret,' Tom would repeatedly tell the others. He enjoyed being the expert — although this was almost all the advice that he could remember to give.

He was right though — plenty of water to flush the blood away. The prostate can bleed a lot when it is cut, and you don't want it to clot and block off the urethra. Drinking plenty of water helps produce more urine, and reduce the risk of clotting.

I was just relieved that none of the men had heart failure. Heart failure means your heart is struggling to pump the blood around your body. If you add more fluid, you put more strain on the heart.

There was only one other piece of advice that Tom managed to remember — and it was a tip I wished he'd forgotten. Tom had the other men so in fear of me that they were distracted about their operations the following day.

As the men spoke about what I was going to do to them, I stood outside their room, hidden. Timing was everything: at the height of the discussion, I burst into the room.

'Okay boys, who's first?'

Silence.

It was six o'clock in the evening and it was time for the boys to have what they had been dreading. It was enema time. I didn't want to give the boys a chance to get away, so I had given them no warning. I entered their room fully armed and ready for action.

The protests began immediately.

'I've just been to the toilet; you don't need to go waving that bloody thing round, you might poke an eye out,' said Tom.

The others followed his example.

'Yes, I've been to the toilet as well; I refuse to have one.'

'You can't force that on me, I have rights.'

The reason for the enema was simple. The doctor didn't want to risk his patients becoming constipated, as this would put pressure on the prostate, and potentially increase post-operative bleeding. (Just for the record, they check your prostate by sticking a finger up your backside.)

When I explained to them that it was either have an enema or the surgeon wouldn't operate, the men soon gave in.

But I still had the difficult job of choosing who to give the enema to first. I knew that if I picked the wrong man, he would kick up a fuss and exaggerate about how uncomfortable the procedure was. Since it was all Tom's fault, I briefly considered doing him first; instead I picked Joe because he seemed the quietest, but sure enough, I picked the wrong man.

'It's blackmail, that's what it is,' he complained as I tried to pry his buttocks apart.

'Stop fighting me and bend your knees up more,' I ordered. 'You're making this much harder than it needs to be.'

I managed to see the target and tried to insert the tube.

'Arrrgh . . . '

I began to squirt the water, hoping to get some inside.

'Arrrgh . . . '

Joes butt cheeks were so tightly clenched, I was miles away from the bull's eye and water was dripping down all over his backside and my gloved hands.

'Joe, just relax and it will be over soon,' I kept on saying.

'Relax,' he said with indignation, 'relax? You lie here and let me stick things up your arse and try to relax. Arrrgh.'

He may have had a point, but I had a job to do. By the time I had finished, more enema fluid had spilt around Joe's buttocks than up his rectum, but I had had enough and so a truce was called.

I pulled back the curtain and my three remaining patients had gone rather pale. I couldn't help but smile. They turned paler still.

The sight of a grinning male nurse with an enema in one hand and a roll of toilet paper in the other must have been pretty frightening.

'That's bloody murder, what you done in there, boy,' said Simon, his voice trembling.

Daryl made the sign of the cross. I imagined bursting into a macabre sort of laugh, but held myself in check.

I approached my next victim — Daryl. He had nowhere to go; he was trapped in the corner.

No one got away that night.

★   ★   ★

Several years after this incident, I found myself in a urological ward in a large London hospital preparing to give some men their pre-surgery enema when the doctor in charge asked me what the hell I was doing.

I explained that this is what we were instructed to do at home.

'That went out with the dark ages; it hasn't been used in years, unless there is a specific need.'

What our surgeon had prescribed was fine, but procedures and protocols change, and some doctors don't change as quickly as others — certainly not quick enough for Joe and the rest of the lads.

Dr Baker

Like most professional environments, in hospital wards you have to learn to work with all sorts of people, even people who may be difficult or even unpleasant to be around. However, sometimes when the work pressure is particularly intense, cordial relationships are not always possible. When this happens in my line of work, everyone can suffer.

Dr Baker had been the head urologist at the hospital for many years. He had worked so long and so hard for the local urology patients that nearly every man over fifty knew of him. The old men only talked good of Dr Baker, and I can't say that I blame them. He was the only urology surgeon that the city had, and he had saved a lot of lives and improved the quality of many more.

The New Zealand government had decided that the urology waiting list needed urgent attention. Many elderly men were pottering around their homes with a tube up their penis for more than a year, and during that year, many of these men had also presented to the local emergency room with blocked catheters, urine infections, bleeding, or a combination of all three.

The solution was simple. We got funding for 40 extra prostate operations, which would need to be performed over three weeks, on top of an already full surgery list.

Forty prostate operations is a huge amount to undertake in three weeks. Performing this many would keep two or even three normal urology surgeons busy for that time. It isn't just a matter of doing the actual surgery; it's also a case of making sure patients recover with as few complications as possible.

The ward only had 26 beds. Considering a common stay for a prostate operation was between four and seven days (and that doesn't take into account the extended stays due to complications such as excessive bleeding or infection), this certainly seemed a tight schedule. It was nice of the government to give us the money, but it would have been nicer still if they'd given us some additional doctors and nursing staff to get us through those three weeks. Instead, all operating fell upon the shoulders of Dr Baker.

Dr Baker went into a prostatic trimming frenzy. He would begin operating at seven in the morning and when five o'clock came around he just kept on snipping away. Time meant nothing to him — he continued to operate well into the night. He reminded me of Dr Frankenstein working feverishly in his lab. The theatre staff said they had never seen him quite like this before, he was manic — and even more-short tempered than usual.

With such a large volume of patients being put through the system, the amount of work for the nursing staff, as well as the junior doctors, was also immense. We were overrun with patients. Everywhere I looked I could see them comparing notes, deciding whose urine looked the least blood stained and whose the most. The old boys were pottering around cautiously, always careful not to stretch their urine bags too far, get tangled up in the tubing, or forget the whole thing altogether. It always made me cringe with sympathy whenever I saw someone forget their catheter bag and then be literally pulled up short by their manhood.

To make matters even worse, we still had other non-urological patients to care for. There were still the odd general surgical patients as well as the medical patients, plus two days a week we had to take new patients from the emergency room. I had a tough job making sure I didn't forget about my non-surgical patients, but there was one person who felt the brunt of the frenzy more than anyone.

Lisa was the urology registrar working under Dr Baker. She had been working for him for six months as part of her surgical rotation and she was having a pretty tough time of it. The problem was not just the work, but because she was female. Everyone knew Dr Baker was irritable with his female staff.

'I can't keep on like this. There's too much work to do for one doctor,' Lisa declared.

Lisa was in tears after the Saturday morning ward round. Lisa wasn't the first and definitely wasn't the last female doctor to cry after a ward round with Dr Baker. At his best, he was barely tolerant of women, but in the event that something was not done his way, then any woman involved would get a verbal battering. I'd sometimes make the same mistake as a female colleague, like leaving the catheter tubing on top of a patient's leg, instead of under it, and he wouldn't say a thing.

No one knew why Dr Baker behaved this way towards female nurses and doctors, although there were plenty of theories. Mine is that he felt women should be subservient to men. I got this impression from the way he would order women to do tasks, but he would ask me politely. At other times he would only ask *me* to do certain jobs, complex jobs which he usually did himself, like flushing blocked catheters. I could easily see Dr Baker working in a ward 20 or 30 years ago, where nurses had firm boundaries to what their jobs entailed, and where the ward sister controlled the place like a military barracks. I could even imagine him having the nurses standing at attention while this god-like being did the ward rounds.

All that really mattered was he made an already challenging job much more difficult and unpleasant.

'I can handle working for such an unpleasant man,' Lisa began, 'but he's left me to do it all. I hardly ever see him.'

Lisa went on to explain that aside from this morning's ward round, she hadn't seen or been in contact with Dr Baker all week. He wouldn't answer her calls, and made no effort to contact her. She felt she had no support and was worried that she would make a mistake.

I asked Lisa if she'd let me tell the other nurses how she felt. She was reluctant at first, but when I explained that she wasn't alone, other female nursing staff had admitted to having problems with Dr Baker, she agreed.

Everyone was furious, and instantly agreed to do their best to help Lisa get through the next three weeks.

The problem was, it wasn't only Lisa who was being affected by Dr Baker's behaviour. The hectic period was shaping up to be just as crazy as we'd imagined, but what we hadn't expected was that Dr Baker would start to act a little crazy himself.

*   *   *

It was late that night that Dr Baker visited to check how his patients were. Well, they were asleep, like all good patients should be at 11 p.m. It was cruel, but I had no choice, so I turned on the light. Two of the old boys never noticed a thing and kept on sleeping, but the other two patients in the room woke with a start.

Dr Baker was keen to check the irrigation system on each of his patients. This system involved a bag of fluids, which were slowly infused up the catheter, flushed around the bladder, and back out the tubing again. The catheter in these cases had two, sometimes three separate channels to allow this to happen. Nearly all Dr Baker's patients had this in place. It wasn't until moving to London that I discovered that this practice was not the standard for everyone any more but usually reserved for the more serious cases where there is heavy bleeding.

Dr Baker always liked to give the tubing a gentle but firm, steady tug. He would then adjust the rate of the intravenous fluids as well as the irrigation fluids before wandering over to the next patient, usually without washing his hands, and having a pull on their tube.

His patients didn't know what was going on. Wouldn't you be a touch confused, waking up in a strange environment to find someone pulling on your private parts?

The last few nights had been bad enough with Dr Baker turning up at 10 p.m. to do a ward round; 11 p.m. was going too far. Dr Baker needed to be told to do his ward rounds at a more appropriate time, but I didn't have the courage to stand up to him.

'Tell the charge nurse,' Sheryl suggested one night at 11 p.m. when Dr Baker had just left. 'She'll have a word with him.' Sheryl had been working on the ward for five years, and was a valued member of the team, but she wasn't ready yet, either, to confront Dr Baker herself.

When we told our charge nurse what was happening, the first thing that came out of her mouth was, 'He's mad.'

She told us we did not have to accompany him on ward rounds at such ridiculous times and promised to speak to him.

Still, however, the following night Dr Baker came around at 11 p.m. and no one had the courage to protest. We weren't sure how he would react to a forward approach, so instead we came up with another strategy that would keep us out of harm's way and prevent us from having to do the ward round.

'He's coming, quickly everyone, move.'

Every nurse in the ward disappeared into the woodwork. Some hid in the sluice room, some in the treatment room, while Sheryl and I hid in the kitchen. Great plan — we were hiding like a bunch of disobedient kids. The girls were even giggling like school children.

In the silence of the night, the clip clop, clip clop, clip clop of Italian designer shoes could be heard restlessly pacing up and down the ward. Suddenly the kitchen door swung open — we were going to be caught! However, by some miracle Dr Baker didn't bother to look behind the door. It must not have occurred to him that anyone would try to hide from him. As the door swung closed there was a collective sigh of relief.

'This is bullshit,' Sheryl said. 'We're supposed to finish at 11 p.m., and I'm not wasting any more of my time.'

She decided she was no longer going to avoid Dr Baker and followed him out. I wanted to stay hidden, but with a morbid sense of curiosity, I crept out to watch the confrontation. It was the least I could do to support her. I wasn't alone; all the nurses crawled out in meagre comradeship.

'We have been instructed not to do rounds with you at these times,' she opened, with impressive assertiveness.

Dr Baker was silent. I almost thought he was going to have a heart attack. His face didn't register anything at first. He took a step closer to Sheryl. I thought for a second that he would hit her.

'You won't have a job after today, none of you will,' he hissed.

Sheryl turned her back on him and walked into the office. The battle was over and Dr Baker stalked off.

The next night, no one knew what to expect: would he turn up late again? Six, seven, eight, nine o'clock went by and he didn't arrive. Things didn't look promising; I felt sure he was going to do his late night rounds again. Ten o'clock passed, then eleven, and still no sign. Dr Baker didn't turn up at all that night. In fact, he didn't come for the next two weeks.

The entire ward workload fell upon Lisa's shoulders. She had to decide who was well enough to go home and how best to treat the complications that surely arise when so many operations are performed.

We did all we could to help her out, but she still came close to breaking down — she would turn up each day looking exhausted, her shoulders slumped, her eyes puffy.

I don't know exactly how but we managed to get through all those operations without anyone dying. When the last of the operating patients was discharged, Lisa promptly quit her job. She headed to a bigger city, where she found a consultant who didn't mind having women on his team and knew how to adhere to the rules. I was pleased to discover she stayed in the surgery field, although not urology; she was one of the bravest and strongest doctors I had ever met.

III

London calling

Following in the footsteps of so many of my friends, I decided to do something that has almost become a rite of passage for young New Zealanders. I went to England. I didn't go there for the best of reasons. I didn't go to further my career, and I didn't even go for the money. I went to join my mates in the great big party city that is London,

The problem with New Zealand is it's so remote, and very expensive to travel to and from. Fortunately, Kiwis can get a two-year working holiday visa to the UK. The goal is to work, travel Europe, then go home and maybe start a family. Once you have a family, you won't be going back to the UK, because very few nurses can afford the thousands of dollars it would take to travel with a family there.

I was even luckier than most of my fellow expats. My friend Chris had a room to rent in Hammersmith. I'd spent six months working with Chris back in New Zealand. She was always telling me how great London was, and how she loved her job. I just hoped I would like it as much. Secretly, I was worried about being out of my depth. I felt confident that I'd learnt how to be a safe, effective nurse, but I was a young nurse with little over two years' experience, and I'd only ever worked in one hospital. Now I was going to be working in new hospitals in a whole new city. Things were going to be very different.

Filling in

I arrived in London and called the nursing agency I was going to be working with for the duration of my stay. The woman on the other end of the phone was called Tracy, and she was to be my main contact person when it came to finding work.

From the moment I had decided to head to London, Tracy's agency had led me, step by step, through everything needed to make this transition happen. They had helped with visa information, nursing council registration, they would have helped me with housing if I'd needed it, and advised which hospitals suited my skills best.

Soon after arriving in the UK, I discovered that there are countless agencies based in London, importing nurses from all over the globe: Singapore, the Philippines, South Africa, Australia and Europe. They all have their own reasons for working in London, but one common link is that most of them do not want a permanent job; the money is just too low.

At that time, hospital staff rates varied from £7 to £10 an hour for a junior nurse. As an agency nurse, I would be starting on £12 an hour.

★ ★ ★

'Well, do you think you're ready?'

Tracy had asked this question several times in the last few days. I didn't know if I ever would be ready, but the holiday was over. Only two weeks in London and I had already gone through half of my savings.

'I've got a night shift in a minor injuries department,' Tracy told me.

I was going to protest. I didn't know much about treating injuries, no matter how minor. One of the most common misconceptions about nursing — apart from the fact that we're all women — is that we know how to treat your common cut, bruise, scrape, burn, etc. While there are nurses who are great at taking care of these things, the average nurse working in a general ward will never see them. We only see the serious stuff that makes it past the emergency room doors and into our ward. The problems I was used to dealing with were things like heart attacks, strokes, chest infections, lung diseases, and on the surgical side, abdominal, vascular and urological surgery. As you can see, it's not particularly practical stuff for out-in-the-community. I hate to say it, but at this stage of my career, the average parent would know more about treating minor cuts and scrapes than me.

But Tracy had more to say.

'It's in south London, not far from where you live. They're really short staffed. They said they don't need a specialist nurse. A ward nurse would be fine. No pressure, but south London is nice. It's quiet. I've heard good things about this hospital. It could mean a line of work for you.'

Tracy had explained that if a place liked you, they would often offer you more work. Eventually, I agreed to take the shift.

★   ★   ★

My watch read 7.40 p.m. I was 20 minutes early. It wasn't planned that way — it was my lack of familiarity with the London transport system. At least I'd be making a good impression. I opened the door to the minor injuries unit, ready to be greeted by grateful staff with warm smiles . . .

'Are you my lover?'

An elderly woman stepped in front of me, her face drawn in a very serious expression, gazing at me, searching for an answer.

'Ah no, excuse me a moment.'

I stepped around her. The department was overflowing with people. Patients were sitting on the floor, in wheelchairs, leaning against walls, even sitting on each other's laps. I waded through the human flotsam, searching for the telltale sign of a uniform, but couldn't find anyone. Okay, that wasn't exactly right. I couldn't miss the two police officers with the very angry looking teenager handcuffed between them.

I made my way towards the reception desk, where I found the receptionist besieged by a group of patients. I tried to slip between the bodies without drawing attention to myself.

'Get to the back,' a voice bellowed at me.

I looked up to see a big man with an angry expression and a child cradled in his arms.

'I'm the night nurse,' I said.

His expression softened and the crowd parted before me.

The receptionist didn't waste time with the niceties.

'Thank God you're here,' she said. 'It's been chaos.'

I considered turning and running as far and fast as I could.

'Where's the nursing staff?'

'You're it. The other nurse went home sick and the agency couldn't get us anyone else at such short notice. I'll show you how to use the computer and put patients into the system.'

Even though this was my first shift in a new country, it seemed a bit strange that the receptionist was the one giving me the handover.

Ten minutes later, I had been shown how the computer worked, where the toilets were, where the treatment room was, where the doctors' room was, and where the main emergency department was in the building next door. Then, I was left on my own.

'I know you're busy, but how much longer do you think we will have to wait?' the police officer asked me.

I didn't really want the police to leave. I didn't want to be left alone, unprotected, facing a sea of impatient patients.

But, I had to start somewhere. I motioned the officer to bring the girl to me.

The girl had received a blow to the head and had some clotted blood on her right temple. I went in search of the doctor to see what he wanted done. I returned five minutes later.

'There seems to be a slight problem,' I confessed to the police officers. 'I can't find the doctor.'

The officers didn't look impressed and sat back down with their charge.

'Are you my lover?' The elderly woman snuck up behind me and caught me by surprise.

'No, I'm not. What can I do for you?'

She didn't answer and went on her way in search of her lover.

'Hey, we've been waiting three hours,' a man called out. 'I don't care if he's a copper.'

The man making the fuss was sitting on the floor, his hand wrapped up in a blood-soaked cloth.

'I'm sorry, really sorry. I'll get to you as soon as I can,' I apologised and went to hide behind the reception desk.

I wasted 15 minutes trying to gain access to the computer system, before I had to give up. I had no idea where to begin. I hadn't even seen anyone yet. I looked over at the pile of patient files and grabbed the first one.

'Mr Fraser,' I called out into the waiting room.

A 19-year-old male stood up, along with two females. One was his girlfriend, the other, a middle-aged woman, his mother. I led them into the treatment room.

'What seems to be the problem?' I asked, as Mr Fraser sat down on the edge of the bed.

'It's a bit personal,' Mr Fraser said. 'Can you close the door?'

I shut the door and pulled the curtains. Mr

Fraser took down his trousers and lay on the bed in his underwear.

'I have a problem with it,' Mr Fraser said.

'It? You mean your penis?' I asked.

'Yeah, it,' he said again.

'Ah, I can ask the ladies to leave if you like.'

I was feeling awkward with the women peering over my shoulder at this man's crotch, so I can only imagine how he felt.

'It's okay. Just fix me up,' he replied.

'What happened to it?'

In response, Mr Fraser took down his underwear and stretched his penis to its full length.

'Can you see it?' he asked.

I had to peer forward.

'I can see a small scratch, Mr Fraser. It doesn't look too serious.'

'Not serious. She bit it!' he said accusingly, looking past me at his girlfriend.

'I didn't do it on purpose,' the young woman pleaded. 'I said I was sorry.'

Back home I had seen two patients with bite wounds who were admitted for intravenous antibiotics. Human bites were quite serious.

'You're going to need to see the doctor,' I said to Mr Fraser. 'You're probably going to need a course of antibiotics.'

Mr Fraser looked at me in surprise. 'You're not the doc?'

I shook my head.

'The doctor seems to be missing. Grab a seat in the waiting room and I'll make sure he sees you as soon as I find him.'

Mr Fraser, his girlfriend and his mother headed back out into the waiting room.

Without a doctor I couldn't do anything that required a prescription. I couldn't even give paracetamol. I went next door to the main emergency department to find out what the hell was going on.

'Who are you?' asked the charge nurse when I wandered into the department. Her name tag read Sister Monroe.

'I'm the nurse in the clinic next door,' I said, not even trying to hide the anger in my voice. 'And I'm all alone, without another nurse, and the doctor seems to be missing.'

The nurse looked about to say something, but I didn't give her a chance. 'The waiting room is full. The police are there. I'm being stalked by a very sweet, but very crazy old woman, and the only patient I saw was happy to show his mother his penis.'

After my rant the charge nurse made a few phone calls to find out what the hell was going on.

'The doctor should be there shortly,' she told me. 'He thought he started at ten. He's a locum. I'm sorry that this has happened. Just hold the fort until the doctor arrives.'

It was 9.15; I decided that honesty was the best strategy.

'Excuse me everyone.'

All eyes turned in my direction.

'We have a bit of a problem tonight.'

I explained the situation to the whole waiting room, from the missing doctor, the inability to

111

get another night nurse, to this being my first ever duty as a nurse in a new country.

'If you really think you need to see the doctor, you're welcome to wait, although it might take another four or five hours to get through everyone. Personally, I would go home and get a good night's sleep.'

It shouldn't come as a surprise that nearly everyone left the department. There were certainly a few disgruntled people, but fortunately no real anger directed at me.

At ten the doctor walked into the department.

'So quiet,' he said, with a smile on his face. 'Should be a nice night.'

The ego

Despite such a brutal first shift, the next two weeks went well. I found work in a mixture of general medical and surgical wards, and while the system was different to what I was used to, the illnesses and treatments were pretty much the same. There was, however, one incident of note.

Mrs Thornton was a very large woman. Every time she sat on the bed the springs would squeal in protest. To get her lying on the bed, I had to grab hold of her legs and lift them up as they were too heavy and swollen with fluid for her to do it herself.

'You're a gem,' she said when I performed this service.

Tracy had managed to find me two weeks of work at one of London's most prestigious hospitals. Mrs Thornton was in the hospital because she had cellulitis of her right calf and was in need of some intravenous antibiotics.

Cellulitis is a bacterial infection of the skin, it generally occurs on the limbs, and it is often triggered by a cut or graze. Unlike a simple cut or graze, it affects the deeper layers of the skin as well. The infection can work its way deeper into the body. It's pretty serious.

I looked at her drug chart.

'There seems to be a slight error' — Mrs Thornton looked worried — 'Oh, it's nothing to

113

worry about, just a slight typing error on the drug chart. Be back in a bit, got to have a chat with the doc.'

'Excuse me,' I said as Dr Hitchcock, the doctor on duty that shift, walked by mé in the corridor.

'I'm in a hurry,' he replied, barely glancing in my direction before continuing past me without stopping.

I had been warned by two of the regular staff nurses to be careful around Dr Hitchcock. He was straight out of Cambridge and didn't listen to the nurses. They said that he thought he was a cut above the nursing staff.

Junior doctors who didn't listen to the nursing staff were a danger, not just to their patients, but the nursing staff as well.

'Excuse me, doctor,' I shouted, chasing after him.

I stepped in his path, forcing him to stop.

'It had better be important,' he said, not even trying to hide the disdain in his voice.

I held the drug chart up for his perusal. 'There seems to be some error with your prescription.'

He began to scowl, and didn't even make any effort to grab the chart.

'It will have to wait. I have more important things to do right now.'

With that he stepped around me and wandered off down the corridor.

I stood there holding the drug chart, wondering what sort of trouble I would get in if I gave the medicine that he had *incorrectly* prescribed, the correct way. I went and checked with Sue, one of the experienced staff nurses.

'Don't do it,' Sue said, without any hesitation. 'You really have to get it fixed. You can't trust anyone, especially not that prick.'

Sue's words surprised me, but made sense. I had to remember that I was in a very big hospital now, and I was a stranger and a temp; no one would support me if I messed up.

I went in search of Dr Hitchcock. I would force him to spend the 30 seconds it would take to correct the error.

Let me explain the problem. The patient, Mrs Thornton, needed antibiotics, which the doctor had prescribed as a deep injection into the thighs or buttocks. The injection is big and has been banned in many places. There is a risk of infection, abscesses, necrosis, plus lots of other things, not forgetting it's very painful. The antibiotic in this case could have been given intravenously, especially as the patient already had an intravenous line in her arm. I could technically have given the injection into the muscle, as it is still allowed in some places, but for me, it felt the wrong thing to do.

I caught up with Dr Hitchcock in the staff office.

'I'm sorry to interrupt,' I said, standing over him as he sat at the desk chatting to one of his colleagues.

He looked up with that same look of annoyance on his face. I placed the drug chart on the desk in front of him.

'I don't want to disturb you unnecessarily' — I tried to keep the sarcasm out of my voice, but I don't think I succeeded because his expression showed even more agitation — 'but this will only take a moment.'

He glanced down at the prescription I indicated. 'What is your problem?' He looked genuinely confused.

'Well, can you please change the antibiotic to intravenous? She's even got a line in already,' I added.

Dr Hitchcock sat there in silence for several seconds, before he eventually responded to my query. 'If a doctor has prescribed it that way, then it is to be given that way.'

With that said he handed me my chart, turned his back on me and continued the conversation with his colleague.

When a nurse gives a medicine that is wrongly prescribed, then that nurse takes some of the blame — actually the nurse can lose their job, while the doctor gets a verbal telling off, so it is important to clarify anything you are unsure of. We all make mistakes, but the way to reduce errors is to be willing to listen to advice. I knew that one day Dr Hitchcock would stuff up, it was only a matter of time, but I was worried that he would stuff up big time now and I would be involved. I have seen an abscess form at the site of a deep injection and I've seen the abscess worsen and eventually cause an infection that affected the whole body.

Half an hour later the registrar, a senior doctor, came to the ward and I wasted no time getting the change I needed.

'No problem,' the registrar said. 'I don't know

why he prescribed it that way, that's very rarely used.'

As the registrar seemed rather friendly, I told him about the problems I had been having with Dr Hitchcock.

'Leave matters with me,' he said, sounding very pissed off, 'I'll have a word with him, right now.'

I wanted to stay and watch the action, but instead went to give Mrs Thornton her now overdue antibiotic.

After dealing with Mrs Thornton, I caught up with Dr Hitchcock again.

'I have another problem.'

It wasn't really a big problem, another minor prescription error, but I couldn't resist hurting the man when he was down.

'What is it now?' he hissed.

'One of your patients has had a bad reaction to the enema you prescribed him.'

'He's had a reaction to an enema?' Dr Hitchcock responded, sounding incredulous, although I can't say I blame him, as I've never seen anyone react to an enema.

I explained what the problem was.

'Well, you did prescribe the thing orally instead of rectally, and it didn't go down too well.'

Dr Hitchcock called me something rather unpleasant but it brought a smile to my face to leave him standing there seething.

Bad news, good porn

'You're a man,' someone said to me when I explained that I was the agency nurse for the afternoon.

'Last time I looked,' I replied.

'I can make good use of a man,' she added, a thoughtful expression on her face.

The woman with the acute observation skills was Stephanie, the charge nurse for the afternoon. I took notes, while she read off a list of patients, their problems, and divvied them up among the four other staff nurses. I waited for my names, but received none.

'Um, Stephanie, you haven't given me any patients.'

Stephanie smiled and nodded her head.

'That's right. I've got a very special patient, just for you.'

'But, one patient?' I added, wondering what exactly she meant by special.

'Oh, don't worry. We meant to cancel you, but never got around to it, so we're one staff up. Don't panic — we treat our agency staff well here.'

The patient Stephanie was going to give me was a young man who was away from home, alone, and had been in hospital for eight days. He had just turned 18.

Stephanie took me to his room and introduced him to me as Jan.

I immediately found myself unable to take my eyes off him — even though I had known what I was going to see. From the whites of his eyes to his bony ankles, Jan was yellow.

'As you can see, he's extremely jaundiced,' Stephanie explained. 'The doctor is very worried about him. We should be getting some test results today.'

I'd seen plenty of adults with Jan's condition, whether due to liver disease, obstruction in the ducts to and from the gall bladder, or cancer, but I had never seen an 18-year-old boy with such discoloured skin.

The yellowish pigmentation you see in jaundice patients is a result of the liver's inability to remove bilirubin. Bilirubin is made up of red blood cells which have naturally broken down. It combines with bile (which is produced in the liver) and is normally excreted in the bowel motion (it's what gives a stool its yellowish/ brown colour). If this process is impeded, the build-up makes the skin turn yellow.

'Hello Jan,' I said.

Jan looked at me with a smile on his face. 'Dzien dobry, hello, hello,' he replied.

'How are you?' I asked.

'Dzien dobry, hello,' he repeated.

I looked over at a sheepish looking Stephanie.

'His English is not the best,' she confessed. 'I think he could do with some male company. He's had nothing but women around since he's been here.'

I knew some people who would pay good money to be surrounded by women all the time, but I suspected Stephanie had a point.

'We have an interpreter coming in about half an hour. The doctor is going to give him the results of the tests he has had done,' Stephanie said before leaving the room.

What does one say, or do, with a yellow-tinted Polish teenager who has very limited English? Speak slowly and loudly.

'I.Am.From.Neeeew.Zeealllaaaand.'

Jan looked at me. His brow was knitted in concentration, but there was no sign of comprehension.

'Do.You.Need.Anything?'

I still saw no indication that he understood, although he was smiling — obviously enjoying the entertainment. I was about to ask something different, when Jan interrupted me.

'You are funny. When the doctor here?'

His English didn't seem so bad after all.

Half an hour later, two women accompanied Stephanie into Jan's room. One had the usual white doctor's coat and was introduced as Dr Brown; the other was dressed in casual, but tidy clothes. Her name was Kasha and she was the Polish interpreter. No one was smiling; in a flash the mood changed from awkward and amusing, to sombre and serious.

'We have the results back from your tests,' Dr Brown said.

Everyone waited while Kasha translated.

Jan nodded his head.

'I'm afraid it isn't good news. You have cancer of your liver.'

After Kasha translated Jan sat there unmoving,

silent, staring ahead.

'Can you treat it?' Jan asked through Kasha.

'We can try. We want to begin treatment tomorrow. I can't promise you anything. It's looking very serious and I'm sorry to say, but there is a chance that treatment may not work.'

Rarely had I heard such blunt words from a doctor. Normally they were a bit more diplomatic, usually waiting until treatment had begun before talking about success or failure. For Dr Brown to be so frank the cancer must be well progressed. Jan seemed to come to a similar conclusion.

'How long have I got?' Jan finally asked Dr Brown.

There was no answer.

I looked at Stephanie, she was staring at the ground. The doctor sat on the bedside and clasped Jan's hand.

'We don't know for sure. The sooner we get started, the better.' The translator stumbled over her words and had to repeat herself. But the answer wasn't good enough for Jan. He again asked how long he had.

I could see Dr Brown struggling with an answer, but Jan again insisted on a time frame.

'Maybe a year. Maybe four months,' Dr Brown finally said. 'But we don't know for sure. You could respond well to treatment. It's just too early to tell.'

Jan's calm exterior cracked and tears streamed down his face. I sat down at the foot of the bed, my legs weak. Stephanie and Kasha sat down as well and grasped Jan's hands in their own. No one spoke.

Eventually Jan's whispered voice filtered through: 'Mum and Dad will be here in two days. Don't tell them anything yet. I don't want them to worry.'

Stephanie, Dr Brown and Kasha made to exit the room.

'Is there anything you need before we go?' Stephanie asked.

After Kasha translated, Jan shook his head. I got off the bed and looked at Stephanie, my eyes pleading don't leave me here.

Ever-observant, Stephanie asked Jan if he wanted me to stay.

Jan looked at me.

'Yes,' Jan replied in English.

Just before Kasha left the room she pulled me aside.

'He understands a lot more English than you think. Stay with him. He likes you, and he shouldn't be alone right now.'

What does one do with a yellow-tinted, Polish teenager who knows a little English, and has just been told he may die within the year? You sit in silence because there is nothing to say. Even if there was, I couldn't be sure exactly how much he would have understood. I got off the bed and turned on the television. I sat with my eyes glued to the screen, waiting for him to make the first move.

'Do you have girlfriend?' he asked me.

His question caught me off guard. 'No. No one will have me.'

I guess he understood because he managed a small smile.

'Do you have one?' I asked in return. He shook his head and managed a small chuckle.

'Not get girlfriend now. Not this colour.'

It was a clever remark, but I didn't find it amusing. I pictured myself in his position, away from all my family, counting my life in months, weeks, days; I'm sure I would never laugh again. Maybe Jan was being brave for my sake. Maybe he needed to be alone after all, so he could let it all out: cry, howl, scream, punch, hit, slam something.

I considered leaving, but then wondered if it might have been me that had the problem?

I'd never been in this situation before. Until then everyone who had died or was expected to die had been old. It was always sad, often unfair and it could be heartbreaking, but it was more acceptable than this, and was easier to cope with.

'It's okay,' Jan said to me. 'It's okay.'

What was he talking about? I got the feeling he was trying to reassure me. Was I being that transparent?

Jan turned his attention to his bedside cabinet; he pulled out a small stack of magazines, and handed me one from the top.

'Good shit,' he said.

I was holding a porn magazine.

The next hour was one of the most unusual of my life, A young Polish man with limited English and a New Zealander with a dreadful, drawling accent tried to rate the talent of each woman on display. When I eventually left I felt, if not exactly happy, at least a little more at peace with the world.

So far, in the few months that I'd been working in London, I had worked with people from all over the world. And, it didn't matter whether people were from deepest Africa, Norway, South America, or any place in between, if a person had a sense of humour, it could make a bad day, good.

Magic medicine

'You won't be having any patients,' said a tall blonde nurse.

Her name was Susan and she seemed very serious. I suppose that wasn't surprising considering the area she worked in.

'It's not that we don't trust your abilities as a nurse, but we don't know you and this is a very specialised area. We can't afford to get things wrong here.'

I nodded my head, and kept a solemn expression on my face. Some nurses might have been offended by being told this, but I took a different view. In fact I couldn't think of a better job; no patients and a full day's pay. I made a mental note to thank Tracy back at the agency for setting me up with this one.

'Fine with me, I'm just here to help out — but what exactly *do* you want me to do then?'

'We need someone to regularly check everyone's observations, their pulse, temp and blood pressure every hour. The patients here can become very unwell very quickly. Is this okay with you?'

I nodded my head.

'Do you have any questions?'

I was worried about how ignorant I would sound, but I had a few that I felt I really did have to ask.

'Susan, this is all very new to me. I mean I've

heard of heart transplants, lung, liver and kidney transplants, but I don't know the faintest thing about bone marrow transplants. I don't even know what sort of things I need to watch out for.'

I was given a quick rundown of cancers of the blood, or in more medical terms, leukaemia. I was also reminded of how susceptible a leukaemia patient is to infection, because the body has very few white blood cells left to defend it.

'Whatever you do, don't be afraid to ask for help,' were Susan's last words.

'I'll be careful,' I promised as I headed towards room I and cautiously opened the door leading into the first patient's room.

'STOP! Don't use that door,' a voice yelled out at me.

I turned around to see Susan gesturing to another door.

'Never walk directly into a room, always use the side room. And always wash your hands and put on a gown.'

I had been wondering why all the rooms seemed to have so many doors.

'Sorry, won't happen again,' I said. I hurriedly shut the door, then headed into the side room to prepare for entry.

By the time I had washed, gowned, gloved and masked up, I was becoming a little worried at what I would find in the room. Exactly how sick was the patient going to be? I peered in through the small window in the door to get a look at the occupant, Mr Tait.

I'd seen some terrible sights in the few short years I'd been nursing, but the sight of Mr Tait's face made me panic — I was certain I was staring into the face of death. His cheeks were grossly sunken and hollowed, the bags under his closed eyes stretched down to his cheeks. His skull was emaciated and his skin was a greenish yellow. My eyes wandered down his body to his chest, where I was looking for movement. I eventually saw some, a very slight rise that told me he was still alive.

Mr Tait's eyes opened and he briefly glanced in my direction then closed them again.

'Water,' he rasped.

There was a jug and an empty glass in front of him. He didn't have the strength to pour for himself so I made myself useful. A thin arm reached out and clasped the glass, then slowly, almost painfully, brought it to his lips. He took his first sip.

'Arrrgh.' His sudden cry literally made me jump.

He glanced up at me again and grimaced . . . no, it wasn't a grimace, he was smiling.

'I look like shit and I feel even worse,' he said to me. 'I would give anything to take away the pain.'

My second lesson of the day: bone marrow transfusions are painful.

'Where's the pain?' I asked, trying to figure out where it could possibly be. The whole body perhaps? Or maybe deep down in his bones?

'My mouth,' he answered.

'Your mouth? What's wrong with your mouth?'

He opened up as wide as he could, and I brought my face close to get a good look. His mouth was a mass of raw, red ulcers, some of which oozed. I pulled back suddenly, trying to make it look as casual as possible.

It seemed Mr Tait could read me like a book: 'It's a side effect of the treatment; they have special medicine for me. Go get me some,' he ordered.

I didn't question him and went in search of Susan. I caught up with her in the treatment room.

'Everything okay?' she asked.

'Well, yeah, I suppose. But Mr Tait's asking for something for his ulcers. He said there's a special medicine?' I explained.

'Oh, that's no problem. Here, take this. This is the mouthwash he's talking about.'

I looked at the label on the bottle of liquid in my hand.

'Ah Susan, are you sure this is right? You want me to give him this as a mouthwash?'

It was unlike any treatment I had ever used — or even heard of being used — in this way before.

'Sure, it's no problem. We use this all the time. We go through heaps of the stuff.'

Mr Tait wasted no time in ordering me to pour him a generous portion.

His drug chart said between five and ten mls, as often as required. He requested ten.

As I poured, I worried what sort of side effect he could experience.

'Um, aren't you supposed to spit it out?' I

asked Mr Tait as instead of spitting out the mouthwash he swallowed it.

'No,' was his monosyllabic reply. He then ordered me to pour another ten mls, which he again swallowed.

The next patient I saw was Mr Henry. He didn't look anywhere near as ill as Mr Tait, but he too had some very nasty mouth ulcers.

'Can you get me some of the mouthwash, they're really bad today?' he asked me as I sat there measuring his observations.

The scene with Mr Tait was repeated.

When I again questioned the swallowing of the medicine, he sounded a trifle offended: 'Of course not. Don't be ridiculous. If you ever end up like me, and I pray you never, you will understand.'

I quickly left the room.

'I understand that your mouth ulcers are particularly painful today, Mr Johnson,' I said.

'Worst they've been for quite some time,' he said, as he showed me just how bad they looked.

I was steadily becoming suspicious but I didn't want to upset another patient and I repeated the cycle again, except this time I refrained from saying anything when he didn't spit out the mouthwash.

The ward had a total of 12 patients and out of those 12, eight had requested mouthwash and five had swallowed it. An hour had gone by and I was back in Mr Tait's room to check his observations again.

'Good to see you again,' said Mr Tait when I walked back in.

Well, he certainly seemed a bit brighter than before.

'You're new here. How you finding it?' Mr Tait still sounded terrible, but he was definitely a bit brighter. I left Mr Tait's room with a nagging feeling that I had messed up. I could only hope no one noticed.

Susan caught up with me before I had a chance to check on Mr Henry.

'The patients seem very cheerful this morning,' she said to me. I had a sinking feeling in my stomach.

'I notice on the drug chart that quite a number of patients have had mouthwash; more than normal, in fact. Have you been making sure the patients spit out their mouthwash?' she asked me. 'After all it is hospital quality cocaine they're using,' she added.

I shook my head.

'Don't believe them, if they tell you they're supposed to swallow it. They try it on with all the new staff.'

Susan left the matter at that, although I swear I could see a hint of a smile at the corners of her lips.

That was the first time I'd seen cocaine used in hospital. In this case, it was the best medicine for the terrible ulcers that are a common side effect of the treatment these patients receive. Apparently nothing works as well as cocaine mouthwash. The medicine is not to be swallowed, but the dosage is actually very small, so no harm done if they do.

A different world

After my first year of nursing in London I knew which wards, or even hospitals, to avoid, as well as knowing which hospitals and wards were great to work in. Fortunately, the nice places outnumbered the bad. But even in the places that I liked, I had to get used to a different style of nursing. Naturally there were always going to be differences in the system I had left behind in New Zealand to the British system.

1. The major difference was the patient to *registered* nurse (RN) ratio. I was used to working with one RN for every six patients. In the UK I often had 10 or 12 patients, with just one nurse assistant to help me.

2. I found it difficult to delegate tasks, especially the unpleasant ones, to a nurse assistant. I was used to doing it all, from the highly skilled stuff, to helping someone off of a commode. It was also hard knowing exactly what each assistant could do as it varied from place to place. I'd find myself doubling up on certain aspects of patient care, such as wound dressings, which some assistants would do, while others wouldn't. Back home, I was used to one nurse assistant for the whole ward.

3. Another shock was working 12-hour shifts. Not all places in London scheduled like this, but most did. Back home I only ever worked an eight-hour shift, maximum. In the UK, if you did a run of three or more days, it sometimes felt like you practically lived at the hospital.

4. I find the small things can make a big difference, so the lack of wheelchair accessible showers in London was a real nuisance. I was used to any patient who could at least sit in a chair being washed in the shower, every day. In London, the few showers I saw in the wards were small, enclosed spaces, often with standing room only. I think this came about because when these hospitals were built, people didn't shower, they bathed. It's not possible to have all of your patients bathe every day. I soon felt I could never get my patients as clean as I would like.

5. I had an ongoing battle with the cleaners; the ones I encountered in London hospitals weren't allowed to clean up vomit, or body fluids, and I wasn't allowed to use their tools (mop and bucket); so, I'd end up wiping up vomit with a towel. I remember trying to open the cupboard where the cleaning equipment was stored, and finding it locked, with the cleaner refusing to open it for me. I don't know exactly how much hospitals save by outsourcing their cleaners

to a separate company, but the ones I met didn't seem to take pride in their work.

6. Then there was the fact that London nursing was truly an international experience. There could easily be two, three, four or more nurses from different nationalities in a single ward, and it was sometimes a challenge to find common ground. Generally the care we provided was the best we could give with the resources we had, but occasionally I'd find things being done in a way that was completely the opposite of what I'd been taught.

7. I had developed some habits in the care of my post-operative patients that I struggled to keep up with in UK hospitals. I was used to all patients who came back from theatre having a complete bed-wash, linen and gown change that evening. I was not alone in not always getting this done, and I found other nurses who felt the same. It wasn't always about the same thing, but a lot of the older nurses confided in me that they didn't get the time to do all the basic things that they had been taught to do.

8. Another habit I had been forced to learn was to keep rooms spotless. I found it frustrating to find patients' rooms cluttered with flowers, chairs, leftover cutlery, magazines, books, dentures, and that's to name but a few things. Whenever I walked

into a bombsite I was always reminded of how messy a nurse *I* used to be, until one day when this all changed. The nurse manager said I needed to be tidy, clear the surfaces, remove spare furniture, because it was a hazard for the night staff. She also said that if there were an emergency, people needed to be able to get into a room quickly. I turned up for work the next morning to find my patient had died, but the arrest team complimented the nurse (me) for having such a clean room, they hadn't had to worry about knocking things over.

Highs and lows of temp nursing

I learnt very quickly that temp nursing is difficult. It wasn't long before the disadvantages appeared to outweigh the advantages. In total I spent four years working in British hospitals. The first two were spent working as a relatively junior nurse on the wards, and after a four-year break back in New Zealand, I returned to London and spent two more years working as an experienced emergency room nurse.

Sometimes I'd spend no more than a day at any given hospital, but if I liked a specific place, or if the nurses in a particular ward liked me, I'd often end up with a line of work.

I've lost count of the different hospitals and wards I've been in, and although it became easier to adjust quickly to a new environment, it was always a challenge.

Highs:

1. I had some very interesting and unusual placements. These included walk-in STD clinics, teenage cancer units, and even sporting events. I ended up learning a little bit about a lot of different things.

2. I was always free to say no. If I didn't like a place, I never had to go back.

3. I always earned more than the regular staff. If you had the training, and could get work in an emergency room or intensive care unit, the night shift paid £30 an hour for a 12-hour shift. You could take home a cool £1,200 after tax for a week's work. But a 65-hour work week isn't sustainable, and the few times I did this, I ended up taking most of the next week off.

4. If you are looking for a permanent job, then temping is a great way to find out which places you'd like to work in, before committing.

Lows:

1. Irregular hours can create havoc with your body. Being able to pick and choose your own work hours may sound great, but you're not really as free as you might think. Work often had its peaks and troughs, and I could easily find myself working two days one week, and in a desperate bid to make up the hours I'd work five, or even six days, the next.

2. When going to a new place, I often felt like half my time was spent looking for equipment, trying to track down elusive doctors, looking for patient medications which never seemed to be on the drug trolley, figuring out which nurses I could turn to for help, or avoiding those who were hostile.

3. As for patient continuity, it doesn't exist for the temp nurse, unless, of course, you get a regular line of work. Having no continuity is not only difficult for the nurse, it's far from ideal for the patient.

4. It's difficult as a temp nurse to figure out what your boundaries are. Some places would let me administer intravenous medications, others wouldn't. Once I was even reprimanded for helping out with a bed sponge because that was the assistant's job, and I was told there were more important things I should be taking care of.

5. It's easy, however, to find yourself out of your depth. On several occasions I ended up in a placement that I did not have the skills for. This usually came about because the hospital desperately needed a physical body to fill a spot, and they'd take any registered nurse as a last resort.

6. You're on your own. You don't get to know your fellow nurses, and you don't form much of a bond with your colleagues. You can feel isolated, and miss being part of a team.

Mrs Olsen

Fortunately agencies also help provide long-term jobs. Often the rates are negotiated. I took my first steady job after my initial year temping.

Tracy had wasted no time in finding me a job for three months. It was on the outskirts of London, quiet, often described as a great place to raise a family. Apart from not being at the family stage of my life just yet, the thought of a quiet place appealed to me.

As part of the job, I would be provided cheap accommodation, only a ten-minute walk from work. I was sold. No more falling asleep on the tube. No more getting lost trying to find the right ward . . . or even the right hospital. No more being woken up at 5.30 a.m. because the agency desperately needed a position filled, even though I had said I wasn't available for work. This job sounded just what I needed.

Alabaster Ward was like any other surgical ward I had worked in before, except for one minor difference . . .

'You'll be looking after beds 1 to 16,' Bethany, the charge nurse explained to me.

'Ah, 16 patients, isn't that a bit much?'

Bethany looked amused at my comment. 'You won't be alone. You'll have a nurse assistant to help you. Orla usually works on your side. She's very good, and knows her job.'

I wasn't reassured.

I didn't like to complain, especially before even starting work, but I was seriously worried. 'But only two registered nurses for 32 patients. It seems a lot of work.'

Bethany genuinely didn't seem to see a problem. I could only assume that this must be all she had ever known. It was the afternoon shift, and this was a common staffing level. The morning shift was a bit easier as there were three registered nurses (RN), bringing the ratio down to about one RN per ten patients, with a nurse assistant each.

I did what every other nurse does when put in a difficult position: I got on with the job and survived, although things were far from perfect. Medication wasn't always on time. Patients were occasionally not ready for theatre when the porter came searching for them, irritating the surgeon by forcing them to wait an extra ten minutes. Patient hygiene wasn't always as good as it could be; having only two showers for the whole ward, neither of them accessible by a wheelchair, didn't help. Wound dressings weren't always dressed as often as they should've been, although I was fortunate to find that Orla was rather proficient at dressing wounds, even though she admitted to me that she wasn't supposed to do them.

Things like feeding patients, walking them, sitting and talking to them were often left to Orla, as I would be busy doing the things that only registered nurses can do, by which I mean giving intravenous medicines and keeping on top of all the intravenous fluids. Or, if a patient was on a blood transfusion, 20-minute observations. Or, if someone was fresh back from theatre, then they required even closer monitoring. When I had the intravenous meds out the way, I had to dole out the oral meds for 16 patients. Often the drug trolley was lacking in several medicines and a drug round could easily be delayed for half an hour trying to track these down.

The list of things to do was endless, but as much as I suffered under the strain, it was always the patients that suffered the most.

★ ★ ★

Within my second week on the job I met Mrs Olsen. She was 45 years old, diabetic, and two weeks earlier had had half her right foot amputated because the circulation had died and the tips of her toes had begun to turn black. Poor circulation is very common in diabetics, often as a result of too many years of having high blood sugar levels, which causes damage to blood vessels.

Mrs Olsen had the most unusual foot surgery I had ever seen. It was as if she had placed her foot under a guillotine and had it amputated, about two inches back from where the base of the toes should have been. What surprised me was that there was no attempt to sew the ends together. I could only presume that this was normal procedure, but every time I dressed her foot it had hardly changed. There was a bloody, open stump of a foot staring at me.

'I don't suppose I could ask you a favour?'

Mrs Olsen didn't often ask for much; she was still fairly independent.

'Sure,' I replied.

'I would give anything for a shower. Do you think it's possible?'

'How long since you had one?' I asked, curious to know if any of the other nurses had taken her to the shower when I wasn't around.

'A week,' she replied. 'I haven't had a proper wash since the operation.'

If making Mrs Olsen happy meant taking the time for a shower, then that is what I was going to do.

I went in search of a chair that would fit in the shower.

Orla intercepted me before I had accomplished the first part of the mission: 'Mr Davenport is back from theatre. The nurse needs to handover now, she's really busy.'

Mr Davenport had just had some of his bowel removed, as well as a large cancerous growth. He had a pump full of morphine, with a cord and a button attached, which he could press to give himself a dose. It's called patient controlled anaesthesia, or PCA.

His observation chart showed that his blood pressure was low and the doctor had ordered ten-minute checks for the next hour. But worst of all was his respiration rate, which was low, because of the morphine. A normal respiration rate is 16 to 18 breaths per minute in an adult. His were ten breaths a minute.

I responded to the low respiration rate by removing the button for the morphine pump

141

from Mr Davenport's hand. I called in my assistant to help as we got him washed, changed the bed, replaced his dressing, all the while keeping an eye on his breathing. By the end of the hour, his respiration rate was up to 12 breaths per minute. It was still on the low side, but high enough to be considered safe.

An hour later I returned to Mrs Olsen.

'I can see you're busy. We'll try the shower another time.'

Mrs Olsen wasn't angry, and didn't seem surprised, although there was obvious disappointment.

'We've still got time. We could even do it in the afternoon.'

I was determined not to let her down.

But I did let Mrs Olsen down that afternoon.

Fortunately, the next day none of my patients were scheduled for theatre.

'Is lunchtime okay?' I asked Mrs Olsen, already knowing what the answer would be.

Mrs Olsen agreed and when lunchtime came around, instead of taking my break, I began preparations for the shower.

I encountered my first obstacle.

'I can't find a chair that will fit in the shower,' I said to Mrs Olsen. 'Do you think you could stand?' I asked.

Mrs Olsen was not deterred.

'As long as you're there to hold me, we'll be fine.'

I wheeled her to the entrance to the shower. I briefly left her sitting there as I went in search of Orla. There was a six-inch step that Mrs Olsen would need to hop over, and I didn't want to risk her falling.

'I'll go at the front, you at the back,' Orla ordered me.

Once she had seen the task in front of us she eagerly joined in.

'You'll be sure to catch her if she falls.' Orla was only half joking, but Mrs Olsen was in fine spirits and thought the whole situation amusing. In fact, this was the most energetic I'd seen her.

With Mrs Olsen squeezed between Orla and me, we got her over the next hurdle and into the cubicle.

'I can't get out,' Orla said, her head peering at me from behind Mrs Olsen's back.

'We can all have a shower together,' said Mrs Olsen, making us all laugh.

'I'm going to squeeze behind you. Suck in,' Orla said, as Mrs Olsen pressed herself against the wall, making just enough room for Orla to squeeze past.

With Orla out of the way, the shower began in earnest. Mrs Olsen rested one hand on my shoulder while she held a black, rubbish-bin bag off the floor. The clean rubbish bag was the most practical thing to use to keep her foot dry.

'That's bliss,' Mrs Olsen crooned. 'Turn it up a bit please.'

I turned the heat up a notch.

'Perfect. I could stay in here all day.'

We stayed for ten minutes, before I wrapped her in towels and, with Orla's help, eased her over the now wet, slippery step and wheeled her back to bed where she could get changed.

'I feel like royalty.'

Mrs Olsen had not stopped at just having a shower. She hadn't put on her old hospital gown and instead put on her own clothes from home. For the first time since I had met her she had make-up on, and perfume. From that moment, it seemed as if Mrs Olsen's perspective had changed. She began focusing on the future, on getting out of this place.

I finally began to see a change in her wound. It did begin to heal. It dried out and slowly crusted over, although it still took a very long time.

Mrs Olsen continued to make an effort with the small things, like putting on some perfume, or her own clothes, a touch of make-up, or doing her hair nicely. She began to ask questions about how she would cope at home, and exactly what resources the hospital would put in place while she recovered. She also made more of an effort to get out of bed. And although she wasn't exactly nimble, she eventually managed to take herself to the shower and wash herself, although I did, of course, make sure everything was set up.

She was a new woman.

A positive attitude can have a huge physical impact on healing. It may not be the happy, positive thoughts that do the healing, but in Mrs Olsen's case, the right attitude helped motivate her to make an extra effort.

MRSA where?

Isabel had been working in Alabaster Ward since she had graduated from college two years earlier. As I had slightly more experience than her and had travelled a bit, she sometimes turned to me for help. I tried to support her whenever I could, but there are some things a man should never be asked to help with.

'Can you please tell her I'm busy?' Isabel begged of me.

She was referring to Mrs Livingstone, quarantined in room 12.

'I don't have time to listen to her stories.'

Mrs Livingstone was in a private room because she had Methicillin Resistant Staphylococcus Aureusor (MRSA). This is the hospital superbug, which is so often being discussed in the media and parliament. It was unknown whether she had the bacteria present before coming in, or if she had acquired it while in hospital, but it soon became apparent that something was wrong after her operation.

Mrs Livingstone had had her right lower leg amputated from below the knee and when it didn't heal and began to ooze pus, swabs of the site came back positive for MRSA.

'But you enjoy her stories,' I said to Isabel, 'and besides, you love the chance to talk French.'

Mrs Livingstone only spoke French with Isabel, because she believed it to be a more cultured language — a sign of class. Looking at Mrs Livingstone sitting in her wheelchair in a public hospital, it was hard to believe she was once a high society woman.

'I must have heard each anecdote a dozen times by now,' Isabel moaned. 'She's very interesting, especially when she talks about the numerous married men she has had. But once she starts, I can't get out the room.'

I promised Isabel that I would share with her the burden of responding to Mrs Livingstone's call bell.

'Oh, it's you,' Mrs Livingstone always said this when I answered her bell. 'Is my nurse available?'

In Mrs Livingstone's mind, Isabel was her own personal nurse and nothing we could say or do would change her way of thinking.

'She's busy right now,' I said. 'Is there something I can help you with?'

'Well, it's not important. Well, maybe it is. I need to ask Isabel something.'

'I can take her a message,' I offered.

'No, it's not that important. Just tell her to come see me when she is finished.' I was promptly dismissed.

'What did she want?' Isabel asked when I saw her next.

'She wouldn't say. Said she would only speak with you. When you're free of course,' I said with a wry smile.

'Don't laugh at me!' Isabel exclaimed. 'She treats me like a favoured servant. You don't know how lucky you are.'

Isabel eventually made the effort to go and see

Mrs Livingstone. She was in there for at least 15 minutes and when she came out, she looked flustered. She grabbed my arm and took me into the office.

'What's wrong?' I asked.

Isabel began to laugh. She laughed so hard she had tears streaming down her face. It was a while before she was in a condition to answer me.

'She's worried about MRSA,' Isabel began.

I nodded my head. 'So? She's had it for a while,' I replied.

Isabel began laughing again.

'She wants to know if it has spread. She wanted to show me . . . '

Isabel paused as the laughter became too much.

'You'd better get to the funny part.'

'I didn't know how to answer her, so I said I would ask you to take a look,' Isabel said, sitting down to catch her breath.

'Where does she think it's spread to? I'm happy to have a look.'

'She wants to know if she has MRSA on her clitoris!'

'What . . . ? Where . . . ? How?' I asked, immediately regretting it, because it set Isabel off into another bout of hysterics.

I didn't go and have a look at Mrs Livingstone's MRSA, although Isabel eventually did.

She said that everything looked fine.

As bizarre as Mrs Livingstone's request may sound, it's very difficult for most people to talk about something so intimate, and so embarrassing. The fact that she made this request of Isabel only emphasised how worried she actually was. And as hilarious as the situation sounds, when your health is concerned, there is no such thing as a silly question.

Deep shit

At 28, I felt I knew a thing or two about nursing. None of the women in front of me looked older than 22 or 23; rather young (at least I thought) to be in charge of a surgical ward.

'Let's get started then, shall we?' said the girl closest to me. She went on to introduce herself as Anna, before pushing a button on the tape recorder in front of her.

Well, this was certainly new.

'Excuse me — ' I began.

'Sshh . . . don't interrupt handover,' Anna said, as everyone else glared at me.

I kept quiet and began taking notes.

The tape recording wasn't the most clear and I was struggling to keep up with the pace of things. I was still writing a patient's name down, while the recording began spouting out important health information. I looked over at my neighbours' notes and noticed that they had a printed sheet with everyone's names.

'Um . . . excuse . . . ' I began again, but was quickly silenced by four sets of eyes glaring at me.

I made do and got down as much information as I could.

'It's a bit different, but it works,' Anna said to me, when the recording had stopped.

'Um, yeah, sorry, but I'm missing quite a bit of information,' I said.

'Oh, you're looking after rooms 1 to 12. Don't worry, Beatrice has been looking after that end. She doesn't like recorded handovers. She'll be here shortly to tell you all you need to know.'

I breathed a sigh of relief.

Beatrice turned up a moment later and began her report, without as much as a glance in my direction.

'Right, let's get started. Won't take long.' She then pulled a slip of paper from a pocket, carefully rearranged the glasses perched on her nose, and began to read.

'Mrs Dickinson, no change. Mrs Truss, no change. Mr Martin has had a good day . . . '

I cleared my throat.

'Excuse me,' I timidly called out.

Beatrice raised her eyes briefly in my direction, then turned back to her slip of paper and continued reading in this manner for all of her 12 patients.

'That's my lot, hope you have a good night,' Beatrice said. She carefully removed her glasses, stood up and left the room.

There was a moment of awkward silence. No one seemed willing to come to my aid. I knew exactly nothing about any of my patients. Anna eventually stood up.

'All right, we'd better get started,' she said. The others followed her out into the corridor. I tagged along as well, just in case I overheard something useful about any of my patients. I quickly caught up with Anna.

'What was that?' I asked.

To my surprise Anna's face turned red.

'Look, I'm sorry, but don't worry' — she actually sounded embarrassed — 'we have a bedside handover next. She'll tell you what you need to know then. Don't worry. I need to get my handover now; you'd better go and get to yours.'

Back at the nurses' station, Beatrice had collected her handbag, put on her cardigan and was about to head out the ward. I cut her off at the door.

'Beatrice, aren't you forgetting something?' I asked.

She looked at me blankly.

'What about the bedside handover?' I added.

She was silent a moment.

'It was all in my report. Said all I've got to say. Nothing further to add.' She paused for a moment. 'Oh, there's a man in room 2, we've put his mattress on the floor. He's been asleep for a while, so I haven't been in to see him recently.'

And with that she stepped around me, out of the door and down the corridor.

I turned towards my colleagues, towards Anna, towards anyone who could help, but everyone had mysteriously disappeared. Either they were hiding, because they were so embarrassed, or at the bedside, getting a handover, which is what I was supposed to be doing.

I didn't even have a complete list of my patients' names. I thought of walking out. It was a dilemma that no nurse should have to be in, but one that happens sometimes: care for myself first, and leave, or care for my patients.

If I did walk out, the hospital would want to find a scapegoat. Everything was against me. First, I was new, second, I was from an agency, and third, if things ever went to court, I could never afford to support myself if I was forced to stop nursing while the case was resolved. It would probably also spell the end of my time in the UK.

Instead, I did what I always do at the start of a shift, and that was to eyeball all my patients, and make sure they were all breathing. I could have gone and read each and every patient's medical file, but decided against it as that would take quite a bit of time.

'Good evening,' I said, as I stood in the doorway to room 1. There was no name on the door and she was one of the patients whose names I had missed.

'Who's there?'

A thin, wavering voice drifted out of the room.

'Is that you, Jim?'

I walked into the room to see a frail, elderly woman sitting on the floor beside her armchair. She looked up as I entered.

'You're not Jim. Who are you?' she asked suspiciously.

'I'm the night nurse. You look like you could do with a hand,' I said, as I bent to pick her up off the floor.

'You're not Jim. Get your hands off me. Help. Help,' she began shouting feebly. I backed off and knelt down beside her.

'It's okay. I'm not Jim, but I'm here to help,' I

152

said in a calm, quiet voice. She sat staring at me in silence. I felt telepathic. I could almost see the turmoil in her mind; the confusion, the indecision, the fear and the desperation. She finally broke the silence.

'Where's Jim?' she asked again, her voice even more uncertain than before.

'I don't know where Jim is. Do you know where you are?'

She looked up at the bed beside her. A full ten seconds passed before she answered.

'I'm in hospital. You're not Jim. Who are you?' She sounded less afraid.

'I'm the night nurse. We need to get you off the floor. Will you let me help you?'

As soon as I said that, she looked behind her, her hands feeling the legs of the chair supporting her.

'Well, it's about time. I've been here long enough. The service in this place is terrible. When's dinner? Have I missed dinner? I'm going to lay a complaint. The service is terrible,' she repeated.

I couldn't have agreed with her more.

The unnamed woman let me help her get up off the floor. She didn't seem to have any injuries and was able to support her own weight. I tucked her into bed.

'You're a good boy, Jim,' she said to me, as I headed out of her room.

I needed to get her checked properly, she could have broken a hip, but I also had to see my other patients.

Everything was quiet, although this could be

because all my patients were dead. It would have been useful to know things like who had had surgery. Or who was going to surgery. I suppose I could ask my patients what was wrong with them, but that approach doesn't tend to instil a sense of confidence.

I entered the next room. This was the guy Beatrice had put on the floor. Mr Mason the name said on the door. I entered the room and was almost knocked over by the stench. I stifled the urge to vomit. Lying on the floor was the cause of the stench.

Mr Mason was lying on his side, on the vinyl next to his mattress; his back was to me, and he was unclothed. Where were his clothes? Why was he naked? In a way, it was just as well he was because he was covered in excrement from head to toe. There was old caked-on faeces that had to be at least several hours old. It was on his face and in his hair. There was fresh solid faeces from the neck down, oh and some loose greenish faeces came out of his back passage right then. The floor was covered in excrement. Oh shit, I was standing in it already. I didn't want to go near him, let alone touch him.

'Help,' he muttered.

I tiptoed around to the other side of the room, to where he could see me. I looked at his face, but he didn't seem to notice me. He was shaking from the cold, but I didn't reach out to touch a limb. He probably had hepatitis C. In fact he probably had the works, hep A, B and C.

'Help,' he called again, still not seeming to see me standing right in front of him.

'Mr Mason,' I called out to him, but he didn't respond. 'Mr Mason,' I said, a lot louder this time.

Mr Mason briefly glanced in my direction, but didn't bother to reply.

Mr Mason was homeless. We've all seen them, even though we try not to, sitting in doorways sipping methylated spirits, sleeping on the pavement, or begging for a penny.

He couldn't have been very old — 35 at most — but his body was emaciated and covered in sores. I could see several oozing sores on the inside of each arm where he had obviously been searching for veins to inject. His hands kept on scratching at them, sometimes drawing fresh blood. His hair was overgrown and tangled. I didn't get too close, in case any of his head lice made the leap over to me. I'm allowed to be revolted, as I'm sure Beatrice was, but that's no excuse for leaving any patient in such a condition. I was going to need some help.

I left the room to track down the two nurse assistants on shift with me.

They were at the other end of the ward, hanging around Anna as she was handing out patient medicines.

'I'm going to need your help,' I said to the two assistants.

They looked to Anna for direction.

'They have to finish their work down this end. I'll send them down your end in a while,' she said.

'We always start at this end. You'll just have to wait a little,' said one of the assistants, obviously emboldened by Anna's words. I looked at the name tag, Susan.

'I'm sorry, but that will have to wait. I need you now,' I said.

Anna wasn't eager to lose her two helpers.

'Is it urgent? Can't it wait? They really need to finish their work down here.'

Work! They were standing around chatting with Anna, while I was literally in deep shit.

'If they don't come with me now I will be leaving,' I threatened.

Anna instructed Susan and her colleague, Melanie, to go with me. They fell into line, dragging their feet and moaning to each other about how overworked and under-appreciated they were.

We stood staring at Mr Mason, in silence, until I eventually broke the ice.

'This looks like your area of expertise,' I said to the two of them. 'I'll leave you to it.'

Both girls looked pale.

'You might want to wash your shoes, Susan. You're not standing in the safest place,' I said.

Susan looked down at her feet and dry retched.

I never could and never would leave dirty work to someone else and besides, these young girls looked completely out of their depth. Gone was their condescending, obnoxious demeanour; all I could see were two very worried, even scared young girls. Susan was only a second year nursing student trying to make some extra money, while Melanie had started working at the hospital three months ago.

'Susan, Melanie, get some gloves, gowns, masks, face shields, waste baskets and a big bowl of water. I'll give you a hand.'

They were so relieved they virtually ran to do my bidding.

'On the count of three, everyone heave. One, two, three, lift,' I said as we tried to raise Mr Mason up into a chair. It was like trying to wrestle with an octopus, as he slipped through our fingers. What was Beatrice thinking putting his mattress on the floor? Cleaning up people like Mr Mason is pretty standard work, if you know what you're doing, but this added complication was proving a real problem.

Mr Mason chose that moment to slip through our grasp and landed in a kneeling position with his forehead touching the floor and his butt pointing in the air.

'Don't move him; clean his back and butt while he's like that,' I told the girls as they got stuck in.

It wasn't the most orthodox technique but it worked. Mr Mason didn't seem to mind; in fact, he appeared to have gone back to sleep.

Forty-five minutes later the room was spotless, with Mr Mason lying on a clean mattress, clean sheets, wearing clean pyjamas and as far as I could tell, completely shit free. The assistants' attitude had changed dramatically. They did everything I asked instantly and without question, but I didn't have time to enjoy their cooperation, because I still had ten other patients to visit.

As I headed home on the bus, I found that I

wasn't tired, despite the long shift. My mind wouldn't stop going over what had happened that night. I kept on thinking about Beatrice and how the negligence of one nurse left a man lying in his own waste.

I vowed to myself to write a factual, but scathing, letter of complaint to the hospital management.

After waking from a fitful sleep that day, I was no longer so sure. The problem was not a simple one, and I even called in sick that next night, in order to think things over.

It was my word — the word of a transient agency nurse — against that of an experienced staff member, with a lifetime of nursing behind her. If I laid a complaint, they would look at not only Beatrice's performance, but my own. They would ask why my evening drugs were given after midnight. They would inquire why I didn't get to my other patients sooner, and ask why I didn't call management when I didn't receive a handover. There were so many ways it could go wrong for me, from not doing my job properly, to asking why I didn't walk out at the start of the shift. That's what management and lawyers are good at, looking back and picking faults, when they've never been confronted with such a situation themselves. They miss the whole caring part of it.

My plea of doing it for the patients, of doing it because I care, probably wouldn't stand up in court. Although I wouldn't have to go to court to be screwed because all I'd need was to lose my registration. That would be more than enough.

In the end, I didn't lay my complaint. I had convinced myself I would end up second best. But a part of me still feels guilty for not. The patients deserved better than they were getting.

Tough love

James couldn't lie flat on the bed because his body wouldn't allow him. Instead, he sat on the edge of the bed, his shoulders hunched forward, trembling hands gripping his knees as he struggled to find the energy to keep himself upright.

'Nothing works,' he managed to say before pausing to get his breath. 'Can't you give me something stronger?'

I nodded my head.

As I listened to his chest, checked his blood pressure, pulse and oxygen levels, my mind had already come to its own conclusions. This 17-year-old boy had neglected himself, and seemed determined to continue to do so.

It was frustrating, because James was asthmatic and a heavy smoker, and he was literally guaranteeing himself a life of lung disease if he continued.

But I could also sympathise with him, because he was only 17, unkempt, in hospital alone, with no family or friends around him. I even felt a little empathy, as I remembered being a teenager and feeling like the world was against me.

I asked James what he normally takes for his asthma, and was presented with a Ventolin inhaler; the most common one around, used to treat an actual asthma attack.

'Is this all you have?' I asked. He just shrugged his shoulders.

'It's what the doctor gave me, and it doesn't work.' He paused for breath, but he sounded angry. 'The doctor's useless.'

I gave the inhaler a shake, and found it to be empty.

'You do know there's nothing in here?'

James scowled at my comment. 'I'm not stupid! But it doesn't work anyway, even when it's full.'

He hadn't had any Ventolin in over a week.

Instead of getting into an argument with him, I got the doctor to quickly prescribe a nebuliser. This is a mask that sits on the face, and provides oxygen, mixed with medication, that the patient can breathe directly into their lungs.

Once this was up and running, I took the opportunity to find out some more about my patient.

'Have you been back to your family doctor, and told him it doesn't work?'

James shook his head.

'Why not?'

'Why would I? His medicine doesn't work.'

I was getting nowhere with this line of discussion, so I changed the topic.

'Have you ever tried a preventer?'

'Don't know. That's my preventer there, isn't it?' he said, referring to his Ventolin inhaler.

It was surprising to see that he knew nothing about his asthma, and while it was also frustrating that he didn't seem to care, it was sad that we weren't going to be able to make any real changes here. We'd get his breathing settled, and then probably send him home, from there it would be up to him to follow up with his family doctor.

'Well, there are actually lots of treatments your doctor could try. And your Ventolin inhaler isn't a preventative — all it can do is relieve the symptoms of an attack. You need to talk about what else is out there with your doctor.'

I explained how dangerous it was to smoke when you had asthma. I even went as far as to say that if he kept on smoking, he was almost guaranteed to end up with lung disease. But I could sense that these words had no effect, after all, they're just words.

I left James alone to give him a chance to mull over what I'd told him. I informed the doctor of how things were.

'When can I go home?' After three hours in the emergency room receiving treatment, James was much improved. His breathing had settled completely, the wheezing in his chest had nearly gone, and he could lie back on the bed and relax. He even dozed off for an hour.

'Where is home, James? Can we call your parents to pick you up?' James explained that he didn't live with his parents, but with a group of students. He didn't want his parents to be involved.

I left him in the doctor's capable hands.

At the end of treatment, the doctor gave the usual advice about the need to stop smoking, and the need to be more proactive in his own care. He also reiterated what I had said earlier, about the deadly combination of smoking and asthma, adding that 80 per cent of people with lung disease were smokers. He was given a new inhaler, and the contact details for an asthma support/education programme.

I was working the following Saturday evening when James presented to the emergency room again. His asthma was playing up, and he was also complaining about how useless the inhaler we had given him was. His problems were exacerbated by the fact he'd developed pneumonia. Generally a young man of James's age would not need to be admitted to hospital for such a diagnosis — he'd be able to be at home while taking antibiotics — but James was too unwell.

'I told you it doesn't work, and you sent me away.' Even though James's anger seemed directed at me, it was really directed at everyone.

'Listen, mate, let's play the blame game later. Right now, we just want to get you better. And you'll have plenty of time to get yourself sorted out, because you're going to be admitted.'

James lifted his head off his chest. 'I'm not staying in this shithole, no way. Just give me some proper medicine, something stronger, like you did last time.'

I tried the honest approach. 'People die from asthma — young people like you. If you have a death wish, you're free to go, right now. We won't stop you.' Amid much moaning and fuss, James let himself be admitted to a medical ward.

When I transferred James to the medical ward, I was pleasantly surprised to see that it was Gwen who was going to take over James's care.

She had been a nurse in the NHS for 25 years, and in the process had managed to raise three teenage sons and one daughter. If anyone could get through to James, it was her. Gwen wasn't one to just do her job, and give out medicines and advice that would most likely be ignored. She did whatever it took to make a change.

James would be sharing a room with three elderly men; two heart attacks and a stroke (no offence intended, but it's not unusual to identify patients by their illnesses). It was James's first time sharing a room, as well as his first time staying in a hospital overnight.

The effect of being in a hospital ward, seeing, hearing, smelling and feeling what it's like, is sometimes enough to bring about a change for the better. It's often a wake-up call. Unfortunately, it seemed to have no impact on James.

After two days of intravenous antibiotics, James hadn't improved. Gwen put it down to the fact that he spent most of his time outside the front door of the hospital, in the cold, smoking. He'd have a cigarette or three, and then wander back to the ward for his next antibiotics or nebuliser. Something had to be done.

Gwen went to James's room and began packing up his things. 'What's going on? Am I being moved?'

Gwen nodded her head, and kept on packing.

'Where am I going?'

'Home, of course.'

James sat stunned. He began to protest, but Gwen cut him off again.

'What're you moaning for, boy? You kicked up

a fuss about coming here. I would've thought you couldn't wait to get out of this place. Or don't you want to get out?'

James was caught off guard by Gwen's attack. 'Ah . . . yeah . . . yeah, I want to get out.'

'Well, at the rate you're going, the only way out of here is in a box. What don't you understand? You're killing yourself. I hope it's quick, for your sake.'

James rallied. 'You can't talk to me like that.'

'Why, does it upset you? Does the truth hurt? Why do you think I'm talking to you like this? Why?'

James was speechless.

'Because we might care, but we can only do so much. You have to start helping yourself. I want to help, but I've got other patients who need my help, and are willing to listen. Are you going to start listening to me from now on?'

James nodded his head. 'I'm sorry,' he finally stammered.

James didn't change overnight.

The real progress began when Gwen took him to visit some of the patients with CORD. This stands for Chronic Obstructive Respiratory Disease.

CORD is a chronic disease of the lungs, meaning, once you've got it, it's there for good. You might have your good days, or your bad days, but as time goes on, it inevitably gets worse.

When Gwen said she hoped his death was quick, she was referring to this disease. Think about running a 100 metre sprint. Now remember how puffed out you were at the end of it. A lot of the people with CORD don't die quickly and they linger for years, for decades even, and constantly feel like they've run a race.

James spent 20 minutes with two patients, Keith, who was only 47 years old, and Bill, who was 70 years old. Bill had been short of breath for the last 30 years, and it looked like Keith might follow in his footsteps; that's if he didn't die quickly via stroke or heart attack.

Within three days of his visit, James was discharged. He'd stopped going outside for cigarettes. He let Gwen set up meetings with the respiratory nurse. He began showing an interest in his treatment and what he could do to prevent an asthma attack. He signed up for the hospital-funded stop smoking programme. He did everything he could to get better, and he got the results he wanted.

Several months later, Gwen received a letter from James. In it he thanked Gwen for helping him turn his life around. He explained that he had managed to completely give up smoking, and also stated that he had only had one mild asthma attack since discharge. The letter was also accompanied by a box of chocolates.

The chocolates were a nice touch, although the real reward for Gwen was in knowing she had saved a young man's life. It would have been easy for the nursing staff to give up on James. They could have just gone through the motions, such as giving him antibiotics and nebulisers, and hoped for the best. Nurses have enough work on their hands with patients that want and appreciate the care they receive, and it's sometimes hard to do that little bit extra for someone who resists.

But nurses like Gwen aren't rare — many will go out of their way to give the best care, even when the patient doesn't want it. They'll do whatever it takes, often that little bit extra (which money can't buy).

How hospitals kill

It's not always a single error that kills. Sometimes its a collection of problems, or conditions, that combine with devastating results. The story of Mr Benson was one of these combinations.

Day 1

Mr Benson shouldn't have been here but there was nowhere else for him to go. He needed to be in a less hurried place, somewhere more relaxed, but most importantly, a place that had the time to give him the care he needed.

The nurse escorting Mr Benson from the emergency room explained that he was suffering from pneumonia. He was 79 years old and normally fit and well with no medical history.

The nurse explained that he was normally independent, and for intravenous antibiotics only, and should be straightforward to look after.

At those words I looked down at Mr Benson, who lay slumped against his pillows, his chin resting on his chest. Like all less able patients, he looked to be in the most uncomfortable position possible. He might normally be independent, but the foul infection nestled at the base of his left lung had sapped his strength.

'I can't thank you enough,' Mr Benson said to

me later, as I was administering his antibiotics, 'you're all so good to me.'

Mr Benson probably didn't realise he shouldn't be here. A glance at the three other men in the room told a story of its own. The sight of intravenous drips, drains, catheters, wound dressings and pumps was not the sort of equipment a medical patient like Mr Benson often needed. This was a surgical ward and I hoped none of these patients would catch Mr Benson's chest infection, or even worse, get a wound infection, from him coughing and spluttering all over the place.

Day 2

I had three patients for theatre today and nine other patients all in varying stages of post-surgery recovery; it was all a bit much.

'I haven't had a decent wash in over a week,' Mrs Jones complained to me. 'When are you going to take me to the shower?'

Mrs Jones was on bed rest for leg ulcers and was desperate to get out of bed.

'Maybe later this morning,' I replied, although I knew I would disappoint her. 'I've got to go to theatre now, it's pretty busy.'

I left her room before she could voice another complaint.

'You're supposed to change my dressing four times a day,' Mr Smith declared. 'It's eleven o'clock and nothing's been done.'

'Sorry, Mr Smith, I'll try to get to you soon.

My patient from theatre is not very well.'

The look on his face softened.

The patient who had just come back from theatre was Mrs Wright. She had lost quite a bit of blood, but was in the process of being transfused, so should be okay. The doctor said that when they opened up her abdomen, the tumour was bigger than expected, but they think they got everything. I was supposed to check on her every half an hour, but sometimes it was nearly an hour before I could make it back.

'My mother has been sitting on the commode for 20 minutes. This place is a disgrace,' said the daughter of Mrs Blake. 'What sort of establishment is this? I'm going to write a complaint.'

'Please do,' I replied as I helped Mrs Blake off the commode and left.

Sometimes as a nurse you may not be allocated a patient one day that you'd had the day before. Even so, I try to keep up to date with how they're doing. I usually poke my head in their room, even if just to say hello.

This was the case for Mr Benson, and I was saddened by what I saw. It was nearly lunchtime and Mr Benson, my pneumonia patient from yesterday, was still in bed. He'd slid down the bed and was hunched in a ball, his shoulders up by his ears and his head on his chest. Why hadn't anyone thought to get him out? I suppose because no one was around to do so.

Sitting at the bedside holding his hand was another hunched figure. Mrs Benson. It should have been a touching scene, but instead it was depressing.

'Good morning, Mr Benson.' He lifted his head off his chest and gave me a smile.

'Oh, good — ' He was interrupted by a bout of coughing that racked his whole body. When it finally passed he spat some foul greenish black sputum into a jar. I had a peep at his drug chart. Sure enough his ten o'clock antibiotics hadn't been given. I didn't have time to give them to him because I was overdue to check on another patient, but there was not another nurse in sight.

Back on my own side of the ward, I was running ten minutes late having decided to administer Mr Benson's antibiotics after all. My next patient, Mrs Wright, needed a fresh unit of blood. I noticed her narcotic infusion was nearly empty, so that would need changing, plus she was due some antibiotics, although to be precise she was an hour overdue for them, but an hour wasn't too bad, at least not in this place. Forty minutes later and Mrs Wright was back on track and everything was up to date.

'Any chance you can do my dressing now?' Mr Smith asked.

He was no longer angry, he sounded almost resigned to his fate.

Day 3

I had the afternoon shift, with a total of 14 patients, none of whom was Mr Benson.

'I'm just going to the other side for a moment,' I explained to Trixie, my nurse assistant for the afternoon. 'Can you please take

171

Mrs Blake off the commode? If her daughter yells at you just tell her to write another complaint.'

Trixie stalked off in the direction of Mrs Blake's room. I had the impression she didn't understand my type of humour. She was only 19 and in her second year of nursing school, and the poor thing seemed overwhelmed. I couldn't help but wonder if this experience would put her off nursing for good.

Trixie shouldn't have to deal with angry patients or family, so I still occasionally had pangs of guilt whenever I sent her off to do an unpleasant job, or deal with a potentially difficult situation. Unfortunately, when you've got such a huge workload, there's no choice.

'Good morning, Mr Benson,' I said, as I entered his bay, expecting to see him still in bed. But Mr Benson was out of bed, and well before lunchtime at that. But it still wasn't looking like a good morning for him. He had slipped so far down his chair that it was only a matter of time before he would end up on the floor. I tried to lift him up but he was too heavy. He was not a particularly big man, but he had no strength to help me.

'I'm stuck,' Mr Benson managed to say, before bursting into a round of coughing. The bout of coughing made him slip further down the chair.

'Hang in there, I'll grab some help.'

There was no one around. Whenever I needed someone it was almost as if everyone went into hiding.

'Excuse me, can you help me a moment?' I

172

asked the lady cleaning the floors. She looked startled; perhaps because I was the first staff member to talk to a cleaner. She remained silent but followed me into the bay. 'I need a hand sitting him up,' I said, indicating Mr Benson.

'I'm not allowed to do that,' she said, 'I'm not trained.'

I was sure I didn't hear right.

'I just need a quick lift, only take a moment. I won't tell.'

Once she made up her mind, she did what she knew to be right and didn't waste any time helping me sit Mr Benson up.

'I'm sorry I didn't help right away. The boss says we shouldn't get involved with the patients. Legal reasons and stuff.'

When the cleaner left Mr Benson clasped my hand.

'You're good to me,' was all he said before succumbing to a bout of coughing.

Day 4

It was the start of the shift, and I made a plea to the nurses to keep an eye on Mr Benson. Everyone agreed to make an extra effort. Claire even put in a request for extra physio.

But this patient needed more than physiotherapy. He needed to be mobilised regularly and not just when the physio came. He needed to be got up out of bed. He needed to not be left slumped in his chair, or forgotten in his bed for hours at a time. He needed his antibiotics on time. He needed to be encouraged to eat and drink. He needed what time wouldn't allow us to give, although we were quite capable of giving, and that was basic nursing care.

I suggested that he be transferred to a medical ward.

Things happen at a slower speed in a medical ward. At the very minimum there's not the hurried rush to get someone to theatre, pick patients up from it, less intravenous fluids to monitor, none of the intensive immediate post-op care. As for skills, it's not unusual for nurses to be specialised in surgery only, or medicine only. I've known many surgical nurses not know what to do when their surgical patients develop medical problems, and vice versa. Fortunately, at that time, I had experience in both.

I found Mrs Benson at her husband's bedside again. In the same seat, and the same position with her head bowed, holding her husband's hand in silence. She had not let anyone know she was here. She couldn't make it every day because she was unable to drive and was reluctant to use the bus because of a fall getting off one a year ago. She couldn't afford a taxi. She had to rely on the warden from the supervised accommodation where she and her husband lived. The warden tried to make a trip to hospital every day, but this was not always possible.

'I've never seen him so frail.'

It was the first time Mrs Benson had actually spoken to me.

I nodded my head and sat down on the side of the bed.

'We're doing all we can. Can I get you anything?' I asked her.

'Tea would be nice.'

I hurried away and got both Mr and Mrs Benson a cup of tea. It was the first time I had managed to sit down with Mr Benson and not be interrupted. There was work I should be doing, but it would have to wait.

Day 5

Mr Benson wasn't my patient today and I only saw him once. He was being wheeled past me in a wheelchair, on his way back from X-ray. He didn't notice me, but I took the chance to look at the results and was disappointed to see there was still a large white area at the base of his lung. I looked at his previous X-ray, taken on admission, and if anything the white area seemed more consolidated. The antibiotics weren't doing their job.

Day 6

Mr Benson had been moved to a single room in the middle of the ward, right in front of the nurses' station. During the night he had developed an extremely high temperature, 39.8° centigrade. Even before I entered his room, I could hear the rattling noises coming from his chest. He no longer smiled, he was too exhausted. When open, his eyes were rheumy, but, most of the time, his eyes were closed. He was drifting in and out of consciousness. His antibiotics had been changed to the strongest that the hospital had to offer, but I didn't think it was going to be enough.

Mrs Benson was sitting at her husband's bedside.

'He's very ill,' I said, as sensitively as I could.

'I know,' she replied. She wasn't crying, but the expression on her face said it all.

'He had a rough night, but we've started him on new antibiotics,' I said.

It was always easier to talk about the treatment than the prognosis. I didn't want to bring up the subject of death, but the right thing to do was to find out if Mrs Benson was aware exactly how sick her husband was and that this was a possibility.

'Hopefully the new antibiotics will help.'

I watched Mrs Benson closely to gauge any reaction. She showed no sign of having heard me.

'We should know soon if they will help,' I added.

She turned her head towards me.

'What do you really think? Please.'

I felt a lump in my throat, but as much as the truth would hurt, I had to tell her.

'It's not looking good,' I began. 'He could get better, but the infection seems to have spread. His whole body is battling it.'

She nodded.

'Is he suffering?' she asked.

I looked over at Mr Benson and his eyes were closed. His temperature was down and even though he looked horrendous, I judged that at the moment he was not suffering.

'He's not in pain,' I said.

'Thank you.'

Day 7

I was allocated Mr Benson today. I asked Claire if we had a resuscitation order for him, but was told not yet because they wanted to wait until another family member was here to discuss the matter.

He was alive. The rattling in his chest was still there. It was a lot quieter, but that wasn't because the infection was improving, but because his breathing was so shallow and irregular. He would breathe two or three slow breaths, and then pause. Mr Benson had no control over this, as he was no longer conscious.

The nurse assistant and I went to turn him on to his other side, and as I placed my hands on his arm and hip he felt cold, lifeless.

We began to roll him from his side and when he was on his back the assistant gasped, 'He's stopped breathing.'

I felt for a pulse, and to my surprise found one.

I ordered the assistant to press the arrest alarm. I didn't want to. Mr Benson should have been left to die in peace, but the choice wasn't mine to make. I placed a bag over his head and began to breathe for him. The arrest team arrived in moments.

The doctor couldn't find a pulse and I was told to commence compressions.

I began to press on Mr Benson's chest and had to clench my stomach as I felt a familiar crack. I don't think I've ever managed to do compressions without breaking a few ribs.

8 p.m.

There were two doctors plus two specialist arrest nurses. They relieved me from the compressions; my arms were tiring. I stood back and watched. It was a shame the doctors couldn't see there was nothing more to do, and ironic that Mr Benson was receiving all this intense attention, from so many people now, when all he needed was a little attention to begin with.

It felt like forever, but finally everything was over, the doctors were defeated. Mr Benson was pronounced dead.

Maybe Mr Benson would have died regardless of the level of care he received. Maybe it was his time. The painful thing is that we never gave him a chance. What would have helped during that week is another registered nurse. Two registered nurses plus a nurse assistant may have been enough to give Mr Benson a chance at survival. Still, I felt guilty.

I felt guilty about Mr Benson's death because I knew that his care could have been better. It was frustrating because I felt that I just couldn't give the care I knew I was capable of giving.

It isn't always like this, with vast numbers of patients to a single nurse, but it has not been an uncommon experience for me. Hospitals have budgets to balance, though I do wonder if they've ever calculated the long-term costs. I hear that billions of pounds are set aside by government to provide compensation for legal cases brought against hospitals by patients and their families, but how much of that would be saved if we employed more staff and reduced workloads?

There would be less burnt-out nurses. There'd be less medical errors. There'd be less staff sick days, and greater retention of staff. There'd also be more time to spend with patients, and to do the simple but vital tasks of caring.

Gotta get out of this place

Mr Benson's death was the beginning of the end for me. To my colleagues, I was unchanged, but inside I was angry at not being able to do the job to my satisfaction. Things finally came to a head one day when we had a staff shortage.

It was the afternoon shift, and again I had beds 1 to 16. The problem was that the regular nurse assistant had called in sick, and they couldn't find a replacement. I bluntly refused to work until they found someone to help me. Claire promised to find me an assistant. So I got to work.

Out of 16 beds, 15 had patients in them, one of them a new admission.

Cubicle 1 — Mrs Wright

A confused elderly lady who thought she was in her own house. She thought her husband was still alive, but occasionally had lucid moments. She was complaining about the pain in her legs, and when she pulled back the covers, I was horrified to see two blue legs. They were the most ischaemic (poor blood supply) legs I'd ever seen. The pain must have been incredible. She had an infusion of heparin (to thin the blood) at the bedside, which was empty.

I promised to get her some analgesia, and get a new infusion of heparin.

It took three minutes to get the morphine ready, and another ten minutes to prepare another heparin infusion, but it took a further ten minutes before a nurse was available to come and check my preparations. By the time I eventually administered the morphine and replaced her infusion, Mrs Wright had been suffering for 25 minutes.

Cubicle 2 — Mr Lewis

Mr Lewis was a below knee amputee due to go home the next day, and wouldn't need much assistance from me. Thank goodness.

Bay 1 — Male six-bedded bay

Bed 1 — A man recovering from bowel surgery and on a liquid only diet.

Bed 2 — A patient recovering from a large gastro-intestinal bleed. He was nil by mouth and on a drip.

Bed 3 — A patient on bed rest because of his leg ulcers, which had been grafted.

Bed 4 — A blocked bowel; nil by mouth, this patient had a tube running up his nose and into his stomach to drain out the contents, and

181

a tube up his penis because the doctor wanted to accurately monitor the fluids going in and out.

Bed 5 — Next to him was a man who was in his second week post a partial resection of the pancreas because of cancer. It was only a matter of time before he died. The longest I had ever seen someone that I was directly involved with live after pancreatic surgery, was six weeks.

Bed 6 — Last, but not least, was a man recovering from a cholecystectomy, or in other words, he had had his gall bladder removed. The surgery is often done using the keyhole technique, but because of complications, in this case he was obese, the surgeon had to do things the old-fashioned way and open him up completely.

There was enough work in that one room alone to keep a registered nurse busy for the whole shift. But there was more.

Bay 2 — Female six-bedded bay

Bed 1 — Mrs Lawrence was 61 and one of the more lively patients. She was always looking out for the other patients in the room and was due to go home soon. She had had her gall bladder removed, and fortunately the keyhole technique had been successful.

Bed 2 — A 25-year-old woman recovering from an appendectomy. Fortunately, she was independent and would be going home in a day or two.

Bed 3 — A 53-year-old woman on intravenous antibiotics for cellulitis of her left calf. Also on bed rest until things got better.

Bed 4 — A blonde, 42-year-old, overweight woman with right upper abdominal pain, awaiting diagnosis. Experience told me this would be gall stones. She had all the risk factors: female, fair, fat and forty.

Bed 5 — A 70-year-old woman with leg ulcers, probably going to need vascular surgery at some point. In the meantime, she was on bed rest with daily leg dressings. Other than a commode, she shouldn't be too much work.

Bed 6 — Located next to the window was Mrs Jackson. At 89 years old, she was the oldest patient in the room. She had been admitted because she had been neglected at the rest home she lived at. The result of that neglect was that she was left with bedsores on her sacrum, hips, elbows and heels. She needed hourly turning at the very minimum, half hourly if possible, but with my workload it was not always done on time.

I checked with Mrs Lawrence in bed 1 when

Mrs Jackson was last turned.

'I'm not sure, it must be at least an hour,' she answered.

With no one to help me I did what I was not supposed to do. I lifted the tiny frame of Mrs Jackson off the bed and turned her on my own. It didn't exactly hurt my back, but I could feel the muscles straining a little as I leant over her bed.

Cubicle 3 — The seriously ill room

Cubicle 3 was closest to the nurses' station and as such, was reserved for the most unwell patients. It had two beds: Bed 1 — My only empty bed. I prayed it stayed that way.

Bed 2 — Mr Peters was 58 years old and had had a huge tumour removed from his abdomen. Surprisingly, the tumour turned out to be benign. Unfortunately, Mr Peters's heart had taken a turn and he had developed chest pains. He was on a heart monitor, and an infusion of medicine to help keep the pain away.

'It's getting lonely in here,' Mr Peters said to me as I walked in the room.

'Well, I hope it stays that way,' I replied.

Mr Peters chuckled at my reply. Incredibly, the bed next to Mr Peters had been empty for the last two days.

Claire walked into the room.

'I've found you some help.'

She sounded cheerful. It seemed she had forgiven me for my outburst back in the staff room.

'She'll be here at five.'

The shift had started at two and it was now four. I should have walked out when I had the chance.

Five o'clock came around and my nurse assistant arrived.

Her name was Grace, and she looked as if she was barely 18. She was nervous. I discovered she was a first year nursing student.

I didn't want to make Grace do anything out of her depth, so I had her check everyone's blood pressure and other vitals.

I was angry, not at Grace, but at the people who had put her here. She was so naïve that she had no idea of the possible danger she could be putting herself in.

While she went to do my requests, I took ten minutes to eat a stale sandwich for dinner, before returning to answer Mr Peters's call bell.

'I've got some company at last,' Mr Peters said, as I entered his room.

Lying in the bed next to him was a middle-aged man with a tube up his nose, a tube coming out of his penis, and an intravenous drip connected to his arm.

I went in search of Claire.

Claire explained that Mr Skove had a bowel obstruction, and was for surgery in the morning. When I asked her if there was anything in particular I needed to know, she told me to read his notes.

I found Mr Skove's notes sitting in a disorganised pile in the nurses' office. I sat and began to read, and the more I read the more worried I became. I went back out to talk to Claire.

'We've got a problem!'

'What's wrong?' she replied.

'Did you know that Mr Skove was supposed to go to theatre tonight?' I said.

She didn't seem surprised.

'Yes, and I was told they changed their plans and he would be going in the morning instead.'

She almost sounded smug with her thorough answer.

'But do you know why they delayed surgery?'

She couldn't admit that she didn't know.

'They've been busy in theatre and decided he could wait until morning.'

It wasn't exactly a lie, but it wasn't the truth either.

'The reason he's not in theatre now is that his haemoglobin is very low. They want to transfuse him three units of blood tonight.'

Claire made herself look even more foolish.

'Of course, he's for blood,' she said, trying to sound as if she knew all along. 'But he's not urgent and they were happy to wait for morning.'

He was urgent, it even said so in the medical notes.

If you ever think things can't get worse, then you're sure to be proved wrong.

There was the slight problem of the blood not

having been prescribed, and no paperwork in the notes indicating that a sample had been sent to the lab to be cross-matched.

The last thing Mr Skove needed was to think his doctor was incompetent. At the front desk I grabbed the phone.

'Who are you calling?' Claire asked me.

'Er, the doctor,' I replied.

'Why?'

I was taken aback. Claire had never questioned why I wanted to use the phone or call a doctor.

'The doctor forgot to prescribe the blood,' I told her. 'I don't even know if the lab has done a cross-match.'

Claire grabbed the phone from my grasp and slammed it down on the desk.

'We do not go chasing doctors,' she ordered me. 'It's the doctor's mistake.'

I felt as if I was having a bad dream; this just couldn't be happening for real.

'We're far too busy to go chasing after doctors and fixing their mistakes,' she added.

'I can't do that,' I said with raised voice. 'I can't not call the doctor, knowing my patient urgently needs blood, knowing he urgently needs to go to theatre.'

Claire tried to speak, but I overrode her.

'This is ridiculous. You can't be serious.'

Claire got up from her seat and came around the desk.

'Don't dare speak to me like that again,' she began, getting ready to let loose, but I interrupted her before her tirade could begin.

187

'You're angry at the way I'm talking? You should be worried about your patient not getting his transfusion and bloody well dying. Why can't you see that?'

'Into my office, now!' Claire yelled. If looks could kill, I would have been struck dead then and there.

It was then I realised my time was up.

I had never before walked out of a job. My error was agreeing to work at all that shift. Over the years I had been working, as well as my time as a student, everyone, from tutors, managers and colleagues, had all said never to put yourself at risk. If it's not a safe environment, don't do it. In reality, nurses often work in less than ideal conditions, uncomplaining, but unhappy with the work environment we find ourselves in. It's easier to plod along and stay quiet than to speak up.

There is a problem with speaking up: ironically, to speak up means *putting yourself at risk*. Management may say 'Why didn't you say something sooner?' To which you will struggle to find an answer. Management will then look at how well you've done your job. They'll see that you weren't perfect. They'll see that things were not always on time, and that some things may not have even been completed. They may even go back over your work records for the past few days, or even weeks, and find all the little faults you've made. In the end you could be the one who is negligent for not reporting a problem sooner.

'I'm off home,' I said to Claire. 'This place is

dangerous enough without you making it worse.'

With those last words, I turned my back and walked out.

As much as my decision to walk out was rash, or brave (still not sure which), it was the first time I'd been stopped from not only doing my job, but doing something that was vital for the health of the patient. Normally I'm trying to catch up, but there's a huge difference between being overwhelmed with the workload, and actively ignoring a medical mistake.

I found out from my fellow nurses that my patient did get his blood that evening. But what if I hadn't pointed out the error and the patient had died? Who would get the blame? The doctor for forgetting to prescribe it? Or the nurse who knew about it, and did nothing because it was the doctor's lapse?

It was at this stage I decided my time in the UK was done. Within two weeks I flew back to New Zealand.

IV

Reality check

What goes through your head when you hear the words psychiatric patient? I wouldn't be surprised if you came up with some rather unpleasant thoughts. I was just a student when I had my first glimpse into the world of the psychiatric patient and like most young males, I was comfortably ignorant — and happy to stay so — of things psychiatric. But, I didn't have much choice — I had to graduate.

I remember very clearly my introduction to Waverly House. It was in my third and final year of training, and this was to be my last placement before my final exams.

As I drove to my first shift, I thought I must have made some mistake. I was in a rather affluent neighbourhood. The houses were big and modern, though nearly all had solid, high protective fences. I wondered if this was because they knew they had a madhouse in their midst. I'd seen enough movies where the psychopathic killer was standing outside the window peering in at a helpless, attractive and soon-to-be-next victim. Obviously these residents had as well.

I missed my destination completely, driving right past. I wasn't expecting the place to be posted with a big sign saying crazies live here, but I thought that somehow it would stand out from the rest. Instead, I found a house just like the others, with a high, solid looking fence, presumably to keep everyone *in*.

Standing on the doorstep, with little idea what to expect, thoughts like would I be safe? or would they follow me home? ran through my head, I imagined someone suddenly opening the door and thrusting their face right up to mine, with eyes bulging, asking what I wanted. The door did open suddenly.

'Ah you must be my student nurse; come in, the kettle has just boiled.'

I was hustled inside and to the kitchen by a tiny little woman who came up to my shoulder. Far from the welcome I had been expecting, I felt stupid for having let my imagination get carried away. She introduced herself as Josie Jones.

The psychiatric halfway house was a place where people with problems could go to spend their day. They could sit around drinking tea, playing pool and join in organised outings run by the two women who worked there. The women were trained nurses, with many years of psychiatric experience behind them. As well as providing a place for people to hang out, they offered counselling and provided a community monitoring service for the local hospital psychiatric unit. They could see who was deteriorating, or not taking medicines, and refer patients to the psychiatrist.

I was next introduced to the other nurse who worked there, Mrs Kelly Scott, and was again surprised to find her easily in her early fifties.

I was wondering where the muscle was around this place — surely they needed the use of a strong man occasionally, to control those patients that became violent. Mrs Scott led me to the lounge where I met Peter, Ben, James and Allan; all local users of the house.

They got up out of their seats to shake my hand and soon had me ensconced in a small circle and Mrs Scott decided it was time to leave.

'I'm sure you boys will have plenty to talk about. I'll catch up with you later.'

I am sure this was a strategy that was used often — leave the new student and see if they sink or swim.

What exactly does one say to a group of psychiatric patients?

'What brings you here?' certainly didn't seem appropriate, nor did, 'How are you?'

Thankfully, James took the lead and instead asked me what *I* was doing there. I was wondering that myself. Before I could think of a safe answer, they started laughing. The beggars were having a joke at my expense.

Allan invited me to the pool room and so our small contingent headed upstairs. The pool room was to turn into the most interesting room in the building. I was told that I would be teamed up with Peter against James and Allan.

As the game got underway Peter began to talk about himself.

'I have schizophrenia, so I don't usually need a partner.'

Again, there was a round of chuckles from the rest of the boys. Peter then explained that he was always hearing voices, he was never alone. He could cope with the voices, as long as they were not too loud and as long as they were not saying anything bad. They didn't seem to affect his pool playing as he sank two balls in a row.

When Allan went to take a shot, he said that he had bipolar disorder, but his medicine was working well at the moment. He sank two balls. When it was James's turn to shoot, he said that he had been an alcoholic and it had affected his brain. He said he was not as sharp as he used to be, as he sank three balls. It seemed the pool table acted almost like some sort of therapy couch, as it gave them an excuse to talk, although I was a bit taken aback at how open and blunt they were. It was also becoming obvious that I would never beat any of them at pool.

Their openness gave me a chance to ask some questions of my own; the first of which was how they could be so open about their problems with a complete stranger.

'We're not all open,' Peter said. 'This is my life. I can either get on with it or spend it trying to hide my problems. That can get a bit tiring.'

Unlike physical medical conditions where there is sometimes a cure, a course of antibiotics or even surgery to solve a problem, mental illness often has no cure.

'But what about your medicine?' I asked.

Peter said his medicine helped reduce the volume and violence of his voices, but they were always there and always would be. He added that at least he didn't look like he had a problem. Surprisingly, this drew another round of laughter.

Aside from joking, I had never before given serious thought as to what a psychiatric patient might look like, but I swear Peter looked like one. He was a small, emaciated looking fellow with big bulging eyes and a large forehead, accentuated by his baldness. He had scraggly, dirty looking shoulder-length hair and an equally scraggly goatee. He was the sort of person whom if you saw in the street, you would make sure to leave a wide berth.

Feeling emboldened by such openness, I asked Peter when he first knew he had a problem. His bulging eyes locked on to mine, and he just stared and did not say a word. I was taken aback, thinking I'd offended him.

When he finally did speak, he spoke with an intensity that made everyone look up and pay attention.

'I knew I had a problem when I found myself standing at the foot of my parents' bed one night with a kitchen knife in my hand.'

I felt a shiver go down my spine. The laughter we had shared earlier now seemed absurd in the context of such a very sobering comment. The lads were still all smiles, but I could feel their eyes looking at me, questioning me, wondering how I would react to such a comment.

'Ah, so what happened?' I asked nervously.

He shrugged his shoulders.

'They're fine,' he said, 'I didn't kill them . . . yet.'

The rest of the group burst into another round of laughter. I tried to join in, as I felt that it was expected of me, but I felt lost. I couldn't figure out what was real and what was not; I guess I must be really fitting in.

I asked him what stopped him and he leant forward, his face close to mine. He had caught me off guard and I didn't have a chance to move away.

'It's as if I had a moment of truth, as if God had given me an instant of clarity, another chance, at the last second.'

It certainly gave me some perspective on all the joking around that had gone on before.

Ben said he suffered from depression and had recently been discharged from hospital, although it wasn't his first time there. He added that he also got a bit excited at times.

'The doctor says I've got a mild case of bipolar disorder, but I'm not so sure,' he said.

'Why do you say that?' I asked reluctantly.

My mind still had an image of Peter standing with a knife at the foot of his parents' bed and I was worried what horror stories Ben had to share.

'Well, it sure doesn't seem minor to me, because I've lost my job, my wife has left me and the only friends I have left are the people in this room.'

He then explained that he blamed everything on one night out on the town several years ago, when he had dressed in women's underwear and gone to the local nightclub, and ended up being arrested by the police.

Many of the people here were like Ben, because they had lost their friends, their wives and children and had nowhere else to go. None of the people here worked, because no employer would take them on. This was their world now and these were their friends.

Spotter

After returning back home from London I didn't want to go back to a regular ward just yet. But I wasn't sure exactly what I wanted to do. I signed on to the hospital register to work as a casual nurse, until I made up my mind about a more permanent role. My first line of work came from the local psychiatric unit.

I had the option of working in a general medical/surgical unit, but I was curious about what it would be like to work in such an unusual area of nursing. At Waverly House I had been a naïve student, and now I was an experienced nurse, but I was still fairly ignorant of things psychiatric, and very curious. My interest was only made greater when other nurses said things like:

'It's not just the patients that are mad; the staff aren't quite right either.'

Or

'It isn't safe' and 'Watch your back.'

The general consensus was that I was making a big mistake.

As the new casual member on the team, I was technically the most junior, but since I had five years' nursing practice behind me, I was actually a lot more experienced than a fair number of the nurses on the ward. There were a lot of graduate nurses, straight from training, many of them with less than six months' experience.

Still, I didn't mind starting at the bottom. This meant being a spotter. I wasn't allocated my own patients yet, and so didn't have to be responsible for anyone. As a spotter, my task was to wander the ward every five, ten or 15 minutes, trying to locate where all the at risk patients were. At risk meant that these people had either harmed themselves, threatened to harm themselves, or were acutely unwell because of their various psychiatric problems. It was a brainless but vital job, and I ended up finding it rather ironic that this often life-saving job was mainly given to all the new, junior staff.

Armed with a clipboard and a list of patients, I would stroll the corridors, hoping like hell that no one on my list went missing. But, of course, occasionally they did. My first missing person was on ten-minute observations and was still absent after 15 minutes. What happens next? Well, you begin by feeling sick to the core of your stomach. You assume the worst. You imagine your patient stiff but not yet cold lying in a pool of blood. You frantically begin searching every corner of the building, the bedrooms, the living rooms, the dining room, the pool room, the toilets, and worst of all the showers. Your heart pounding in your chest as you open the door to the showers, a large, bare space with five closed doors facing you, desperately hoping your missing patient is not hanging around in one of the cubicles. Opening each shower door is like a terrible lottery: *And behind door number three is Mr Smith, freshly hanged and still warm to touch.*

I found the patient half an hour later. One of the new graduate nurses had foolishly taken him outside for a breath of fresh air. Not only was he not supposed to be outside, she had not told anyone that she was taking him.

But it can go other ways.

One patient, who I came to know reasonably well during my 18 months in the psychiatric unit, had made eight attempts to kill herself, two of those in the previous 12 months. After eight attempts, you might think she wasn't quite sincere about wanting to finish her life, but she was, she was just plain unlucky (or lucky, depending on your point of view).

She had tried gassing herself in her garage, using her car. Her neighbours had broken in to find her semiconscious.

She had taken three overdoses, each attempt more potentially lethal than the last. She began with Prozac, then paracetamol and finally tricyclic antidepressants, which have a rather nasty habit of affecting the heart rhythm.

She had cut her wrists a couple of times and been found again by her neighbours. I wouldn't have been surprised if her neighbours ended up admitting themselves.

She had also hanged herself twice. The last attempt while an inpatient in our unit. She was on the spotter list and she was found to be missing (thankfully, I was not on spotter duty at the time).

It was nine o'clock at night and pitch black outside; everyone just hoped that she was somewhere inside, otherwise there would be no chance of finding her. As we raced around the unit searching, I heard a scream, followed by yells for help coming from the bathroom.

It's horrifying, but curiously amazing, what people manage to hang themselves on. This patient had managed to hang herself from a door handle, with the use of a shoe lace. The door handle attempt worked and she died. The nurse looking after her that shift was not blamed, but The System was. The System let her down and subsequently more stringent regulations were put into effect, to prevent this happening again, or so I've been told.

Someone who has made eight pretty good attempts on their life is eventually going to get it right. She was on a five-minute watch, but if someone can be so inventive in their determination to kill themselves, then no matter what safeguards we put in place they would find a way around them.

Mr Townsend

Despite the tragedies I was fascinated by mental health. My colleagues back in the medical ward — or real nursing world, as they liked to consider it — continued to think I was mad for doing what I was doing. In some respects I could understand their position.

It wasn't real work as they knew it. There were no patients to wash, no wounds to dress, no one to rush to theatre. Instead of the physical things I had previously considered to be the biggest part of nursing, I was learning to listen.

'What's wrong, Mr Townsend?' I asked.

Mr Townsend was sitting on his bed with his head in his hands, rocking back and forth.

'I'm sick of fighting them,' he said as he pulled his hands away, wiping the moisture from the corner of his eyes.

'What have they said this time?' I asked.

I had been instructed that this was the wrong thing to say. Delving into people's delusions only reinforces them, but sometimes you need to understand what you're dealing with. Personally I think it's a balancing act; you need to know enough about what's troubling them to help them, yet at the same time not to dig too deep, or too often.

At 55, Mr Townsend had spent over 30 years wrestling with the voices in his head.

'They want me to put a fork in the electrical

socket . . . I don't want to do it. I just want them to stop,' he pleaded.

I've seen people survive electrical shocks, but not always and it certainly has to be one of the more unpleasant ways to die. I imagined Mr Townsend with a piece of cutlery in the plug hole, his body convulsing as the current surged through him, his hand turning black and smoke rising from his flesh.

'Do you want some more meds?' I asked.

'Please,' he begged.

I went and got him something to relax him. The treatment never got rid of the voices, just moved them into the background a bit, where he was able to ignore them for a while. If it wasn't the electrical socket, it was some other way for Mr Townsend to hurt or kill himself.

Mr Townsend seemed to spend as much time in hospital as out. He was a familiar face in the ward, and his delusions usually had the same theme. They generally involved voices telling him to hurt himself in one way or another. As far I'm aware, his voices never told him to hurt anyone else, although you can never be sure.

Once, when Mr Townsend had been reasonably lucid, he had explained that he knew he shouldn't do the things the voices said, but sometimes he got confused as to what was real and what was not. Mr Townsend said that by talking to the nurses, it helped distract him from the voices in his head.

Dan's demons

Out of all the madness and chaos that became an everyday part of the job, there was one patient who stood out from the rest. Dan was 16, the youngest patient in the ward, and also one of the saddest cases I had ever seen. Dan lived somewhere else, and it took me four months to get a glimpse of that world.

Dan spent much of his day walking up and down the length of the corridor, on autopilot, smiling to himself. His was almost a caricature of an insane smile, devoid of warmth or humour. Sometimes he would even laugh for a brief second, then quickly stifle it if he realised that he had been heard.

For my first few months in the ward, Dan wouldn't speak to me. When I'd say hello, he would just walk on as if he hadn't heard a thing. There were a couple of times when his eyes would lock on to mine, but I didn't like it when he stared at me. His pupils were always so big, as if struggling to cope with all that they were seeing. When I looked into his eyes, it was sometimes hard to see anything human in there; other times, all I could see was a suffering kid. Even when he stared, he didn't really seem to see me; he was distracted, frightened and alone.

All I knew about Dan's family history was that he was the youngest of nine children, from the poorest part of our town. He had done what a lot of pre-adolescent children did in that neighbour-hood, and began smoking marijuana when he was 12. The doctors believed Dan may have begun to hear voices from as young as 14, although he wasn't officially diagnosed with schizophrenia until he was 15. At the start he only heard voices when he smoked a joint. Then as his use increased, so did the frequency and severity of his symptoms. To me, it didn't take a scientific genius to see the link between Dan's smoking and his illness.

It took Dan a long time to work up the courage to talk to me; he must have been pretty suspicious of me, as I was a new face and probably a threat to him, at least in his mind. Our first conversation came about in a rather unexpected way.

'What the fuck are you looking at?'

Okay, it may not sound like much of a conversation, but it was genuinely the first time he had spoken to me. The ice had been broken and things rapidly warmed between us. Subsequent conversations extended to, 'Hello' and 'Goodbye.'

I soon realised I would never be able to have an even remotely normal conversation with Dan. He was constantly trying to cope with at least two conversations at once. His mind would wander from one topic to the next, unable to focus for too long on anything I said. The only thing he could focus on were the demons in his head and those sitting beside me.

As Dan gradually became more comfortable with my presence, he began to trust me. One day he decided to open up completely with me. It was as if a switch had been flicked inside his head — I was no longer an outsider, no longer someone to be feared, instead I had become a small part of his world, like a piece of furniture that he was now comfortable using.

'There's a black demon sitting next to you,' he told me. 'He's got red eyes. He says you're a fucking cunt.'

I glanced briefly over my left then right shoulder, knowing I'd see nothing, but unable to help myself. Despite our instructions not to question people about their delusions, I couldn't help myself asking what this demon was saying about me.

'Kiss my arse, fuck-head; you're going to burn in hell. He wants me to punch you in the head.'

I had to remind myself that Dan was just repeating what the demon had said to him. Dan was smiling that humourless smile.

I felt vulnerable, sitting there facing a truly psychotic patient. I had goosebumps on my arms. I had an awful thought, imagining that what Dan could see was real, and it was I who was unable to see what was really there. But such thoughts are too scary to contemplate; at this rate I would be admitting myself as a patient.

As Dan's trust in me grew, I thought I would put it to good use. Over the past couple of weeks, I had been getting patients to join in activities outside of the building. It was nothing special, just kicking a football around, but it made a welcome break from sitting in the lounge watching television — a television that was probably broadcasting secret messages into everyone's head — plus the patients seemed to love it.

Dan had not been outside the unit in over three months. He was scared of something.

I got him as far as the door before he had a change of mind.

'I don't want to play. Football is a stupid game,' he said.

'Why don't you try standing by the doorway?' I suggested. If I could get him outside I felt sure I could get him to eventually join in. 'You don't have to play, just watch. You can always go back inside if you don't like it.'

Dan reluctantly followed me out. Many of the staff came out as well, just to see for themselves that Dan had made it outside.

At first Dan stood by the door, watching everyone else kick the ball around, when suddenly he just bolted, straight out into the middle of the field, straight after the football. He wasn't interested in choosing sides; he just wanted the ball for himself. No matter who had the ball, he went after them. Dan laughed — the first genuine, normal laugh anyone had heard from him. I could see patients and staff alike affected; we were all grinning from ear to ear.

But the next day Dan would not come outside; he wouldn't even get out of bed. He lay curled up in his blankets, the sheet wrapped around his head with only a tiny gap where I could see two eyes staring out at me. Those eyes showed absolute terror.

'They're going to get me,' Dan said by way of welcome.

'Who's going to get you, Dan? What's going to get you?'

Stupid of me. I'd just strengthened his delusion; I should have said 'No one is going to get you.' I needed to think before I spoke. I did get an answer.

'The dogs are going to get me! I can hear them outside, barking, snarling; waiting for me.'

I tried to persuade him to at least get out of bed.

'We won't go outside. We'll just get out of bed. The dogs are outside, not inside.'

I silently berated myself; I kept saying the wrong thing. I'd just reinforced his belief that the dogs were outside. I meant well but I knew I was causing more harm than good.

'Fuck no! Are you crazy?'

Dan was almost shouting at me now. He seemed frustrated that I couldn't seem to understand him.

'Listen, Dan, let's just try sitting on the edge of the bed. I'll sit with you. Nothing is going to happen.'

'Can't you see them?' He had lowered his voice, but the terror was still coming through loud and clear. 'They're everywhere, all over the place. Fuck, they're on me.' He began to raise his voice again. 'They're on me,' he repeated. 'Do something.'

I didn't know what to do. I was as confused as he was. I wanted to help, but I only felt completely useless.

'The spiders are everywhere,' he shouted. 'I can feel them crawling on me. I can feel them biting me.'

His voice was becoming less coherent as he became more excited. I was at a loss at what to do and so I called the doctor.

Dan was given more medicine, and although it didn't alter his belief in his reality, it did relax him enough that he did manage to get out of bed with a lot of persuasion and a promise that I would stay with him. I also promised him that nothing would happen to him. Another stupid thing to say; all medical people know not to promise anything.

As we began walking along the main corridor Dan suddenly slumped to the left. He couldn't lift his left arm and his left shoulder was 12 inches lower than the right.

Dan looked at me and said, 'Why am I walking like this?'

I knew why, this was a side effect from all the medication he had been given. I even knew the name given to these side effects: extrapyramidal. I was still surprised at such a sudden and dramatic onset of symptoms, especially as I had never seen anything so severe as this before.

Extrapyramidal side effects are a common result of taking antipsychotic medication. They can take the form of tremors, restlessness, sudden contractions of a muscle, or even group of muscles. Some can be life threatening. The most common side effects I had seen were rolling of the tongue and tremor in the limbs.

Dan received further medicine, an injection

this time, to counter the extrapyramidal side effects and to our immense relief his symptoms disappeared.

It seemed ironic to think that it was drugs that had triggered Dan's schizophrenia and here we were pumping him full of more drugs. It also seemed strange to think that many people take drugs to achieve the sort of effects that Dan had, but still we gave Dan more. For all the drugs we gave Dan, we didn't seem to make a positive difference. Instead, we gave him side effects. It was just as well we had drugs to treat the side effects, too.

I am not discounting the value of psychiatric medicine, because it does make a huge difference for some and it does allow many people to lead normal lives, but with Dan nothing seemed to work. Dan was eventually placed in a long-term community house with 24-hour supervision. He would never be able to look after himself and I cannot see a cure in the near future. Dan's life was and will always be a battle between what is real and what is delusion, although it seemed that battle was already lost for Dan.

As time in the psychiatric unit went by, I truly began to appreciate how powerful the mind is. Here the mind reigned supreme. It was strange to see people without physical problems — no obvious deformity, no missing limbs, no failing body parts — often somehow worse off than those with. To see a young man or woman ruined by the thoughts running through their head is terrifying.

Mr Brown

The front door slammed open and crashed against the wall. All the staff heard the noise and came running to the reception area, where Mr Brown was being carried in through the front door. He was a big, strong, healthy looking man, perfectly capable of walking. But it is rather hard to walk when your feet and arms are handcuffed.

'Don't just stand there,' the police officer in charge said, noticing me staring. 'Lend us a hand.'

As he spoke, the man in handcuffs suddenly jerked his body to the right, sending the officer on that side crashing into the wall.

The only coherent words that could be heard from all the shouting were 'fuck' and 'kill' from Mr Brown. I leapt into the fray, grabbing hold of his wrists by the handcuffs.

As I pulled the patient along, I got my first close-up glimpse of him. His eyes were red and watering from the pepper spray the police had used to subdue him. Despite this, he was putting up quite a struggle, writhing, almost spasming in our grasp. As we carried him towards the seclusion room, he threw all his weight again, this time to the left, and managed to end up on the floor. The unexpected movement ripped the handcuffs from my hands and left me with a few less layers of skin. This was rapidly looking to be the most violent, acutely psychotic patient I had seen yet. It was an intimidating sight.

As we picked the patient up off the floor I heard a shout from one of the officers: 'Fuck!'

As he had leant forward to pick up Mr Brown, he had left his arm exposed within reach of Mr Brown's mouth, and he hadn't wasted a chance to sink his teeth into flesh. The skin was broken, but at least there wasn't a chunk of flesh missing.

We took Mr Brown into the seclusion room. This barren room with a solid wood door with several locks was our answer to those whose energies got out of control. The room was designed to prevent the patient causing themselves harm; it also helped to provide staff and other patients with a safe environment. The room was meagrely furnished, with a thick plastic mattress and a paper bucket to use as a toilet, along with a paper cup full of water. Any patient placed in this room was stripped of their clothing and dressed in a thickly woven gown that was impossible to tie into knots, meaning there was no way a patient could strangle him or herself with it.

'He nearly killed one of us before,' the officer in charge remarked.

The next trick was to remove the handcuffs and escape in one piece.

The leg handcuffs came off first, and Mr Brown remained still.

'Watch him, boys,' the officer in charge warned. 'He's just waiting for his hands to be free.'

He was brought down to the ground, face first. In this position he wouldn't be able to use his arms to hit us as the handcuffs were removed.

There was nothing more we could do until the psychiatrist arrived, which we had been told would be in about 15 minutes. It was time to leave. I instructed the officers holding the legs to go first, then next the officers holding the hands, followed very quickly by me. The secret to a safe exit is simple: move as fast as you bloody well can, slam the door and lock the bolts.

As the bolts were thrown home, Mr Brown charged for the door pounding on it with fists and feet for several minutes, before giving up and sitting back down on the mattress, staring at the door.

'I think he needs a male to look after him,' said the charge nurse, kindly volunteering my services.

The police left and I was given the job of sitting outside the seclusion room door and peering in through the tiny reinforced window every five minutes. An urgent call had gone out for the psychiatrist to come as soon as possible. Mr Brown needed some serious sedation; his mind and body needed to rest.

As we waited, Mr Brown came to stand by the door, inches from where I sat, and tried to plead with me to let him go.

'I'll be good now. You can trust me. I'll do as you say. You can even open the door and I'll just sit here. Just open the door, that's all.'

I ignored him. It wasn't long before he changed tactics.

'Let me out, or I'll fucking kill you. You'll be

the first. I'll make it hurt. Let me out now and you'll live. Do you want to die? You're gonna die, with my hands around your throat.'

He began to kick the door, the old wood taking a hell of a battering. I checked all three locks, to make sure they were all bolted securely. I endured several minutes of some very graphic abuse, before he tried the pleading tactic again. In total I suffered 20 minutes of this barrage of begging and threatening, before the psychiatrist arrived.

Dr King took one look in through the window and ordered a very strong dose of tranquilliser.

'He does appear to be in a very bad way, wouldn't you say?' he asked casually.

I wasn't sure if he expected an answer or not.

'You sort out Mr Brown and I'll draw up the injection,' Dr King ordered.

He didn't appear to be the least bit worried by the situation. Of course, at the age of 59, he would have no hand in the upcoming restraint.

The problem now was how to get in there and administer the injection. Since the police had left, I had to ask the staff to assist me and I was sure that help would not be forthcoming. For a start, I was the only male on that shift and, second, the average age of the women was at least 40.

'Um, I've got a bad back; hurt it during my last restraint,' said Jane, the only nurse my age.

The other women didn't even bother with an excuse; they said flat out that they did not have a death wish. I had no option but to call in the police.

Before long, the same four officers who had brought Mr Brown in were beside me, peering at the patient who had by now realised we were coming. If there had ever been any notion that Mr Brown was going to make things easy for us, and that he might have calmed down a bit, his shadow boxing performance soon put an end to it. It seemed as if madness had lent strength to Mr Brown.

I motioned for the officers to lead the way.

The officer in charge, Sergeant Perkins, looked at me and said, 'He's your bloody patient; you go first.'

It had been worth a try.

There is a strategy we use when taking down a violent patient, it involves each person being designated a specific body part, that is, right arm, left arm, right leg, left leg or head. If you are responsible for a body part then that is all you aim for. This strategy requires feeling confident that your partners do their job and concentrate on their body parts. If I was to grab Mr Brown's right arm but my partner was to fail to take the left arm I would end up with a very swift hook to the side of the head. It's all about trust.

It's also about speed; we needed to try to overwhelm Mr Brown with speed and organisation. The door was opened quickly (which was actually rather hard since it had three locks) and I led the charge, my head down and my eyes glued to Mr Brown's right arm. I caught a couple of glancing blows to the shoulder and head, but luckily nothing connected properly and soon we had his arms and legs pinned. The last officer came in and supported the patient's head and we slowly lowered him to the ground. We had done a good job; we had our man immobilised and no one was hurt — not even the patient.

As we lay there, the doctor calmly waltzed in and complimented us on such a nice takedown. He jabbed a very big injection into Mr Brown's buttocks, then calmly removed himself from the room. It was now time for us to make our exit.

At least this time I wasn't the last out. The two lads restraining the legs exited first, and then Sergeant Perkins and I left, as we had the arms, followed very closely by the last officer who had held the head. The door slammed shut and the bolts were thrown across. Mr Brown didn't bother to get up; he just lay there staring at the wall.

It's pretty hard to forget some of the more colourful characters and even harder to forget some of the more violent ones. It is an unfortunate fact that violence is not uncommon in a psychiatric ward, whether it is to oneself or to others. Some days it seemed as if the unit was a big cauldron, brimming with pent-up anger and excitement. Such strong emotions, such raw energy, are not easily diffused in a closed environment; they have nowhere to go.

As I resumed my vigil outside Mr Brown's room, I thought about how having another male or two in this place would help. Thankfully the unit eventually hired a full-time muscle man, a giant of a guy that even a crazed patient would think twice about crossing. Some nurses felt this was not needed and sexist; I just thought it common sense.

Food for thought

Jeneil had walked at least half a dozen lengths of the ward, and it was time to put a stop to it. The problem was I'd never had a confrontation with her. Thus far, our working relationship had been polite, brief, and very superficial. The nurses never allocated Jeneil to me as I was still relatively inexperienced. I lacked the knowledge necessary to deal with the complexity of an anorexic patient, but today was different. Due to a shortage of staff, my name had been put on the board next to Jeneil's.

'How're things?' I asked her as I trotted alongside. She was walking at a cracking pace, and I was nearly jogging to keep up.

'Fine, and you?' she replied.

'Good, good, although today's a bit different. I'm your designated nurse for today.'

Jeneil gave me a big smile.

'Then it'll be an easy day for you. You don't have to do anything for me. I can take care of myself.'

Her words stressed how out of contact with reality she was. She was a walking skeleton. Jeneil looked so frail and thin, a stiff breeze might knock her over, and the fall would break every brittle bone in her body. She had fur on her limbs and face — fine, soft white hair that covered her like a soft, silvery white coat, which grows because the body needs to provide some insulation since the patient no longer has fat stores to help keep them warm. Marching like this was one of the tactics she used to lose weight when confined to the ward.

'Well . . . ' I paused, trying to find a safe way to say what I needed to, without sounding confrontational, but it just wasn't possible. 'I'm sorry, but you're going to have to stop walking.'

She began to walk faster.

'Who are you to tell me what to do? Just stay out of my way.'

I had seen what my colleagues had done in the past if she wouldn't cooperate, but I didn't want to have to confine her to her room.

'You know the rules, Jeneil, and besides, you agreed you'd go along with them,' I reminded her.

Jeneil reached the end of the ward and did an about turn. I again found myself playing catch-up. We walked in silence for another length of the ward. She suddenly stopped and turned towards me, her mask of polite civility was gone, her eyes were smouldering.

'You don't know me. You're new here, and you think you know how to help me. Is that what you're trying to do, help me?' Her voice began to climb an octave or two. 'You don't know a thing, and besides, we all know you're struggling anyway. This place isn't for you. Get out before you hurt someone.'

I had been told that anorexia sufferers could be very manipulative, but I was not prepared for how cutting Jeneil's comment was.

This was a huge change from the chats we'd

had before — conversations about the weather, news, events — although at the time, even these had felt strange; it was odd to happily chat away, all the while ignoring the matter of her weight.

'Well, if that's the way you feel, I'll get someone to take over your care for today.'

Jeneil didn't respond, but went to the lounge and sat down in front of the television. I retreated to the nurses' station.

'She's got a sharp tongue, hasn't she?' remarked Mary, one of the senior nurses on that day. Mary had spent 20 years working in psychiatry, and she'd dealt with many people like Jeneil.

'It caught me off guard, that's for sure,' I replied.

'Don't argue with her, just stay calm, and be firm. If you have any doubts, she'll sense them, and tear you apart.'

She was right, of course, but what disturbed me the most was how rational, nice and intelligent Jeneil was when she wasn't confronted. It was so sad. I still didn't understand how someone so sweet could be so messed up. I went home hoping that I would not have to look after Jeneil the next day.

The following morning I found Jeneil confined to her room; in fact, not only confined, but on bed rest. Mary, who was sitting by her side, stood up, and motioned for me to follow her outside the room.

'She's dropped below her minimum weight, so she's confined to her bed,' Mary explained.

Jeneil's target weight was 45 kilograms, and

she was now 44. Jeneil could manipulate her weight as easily as she could people. She could gain or lose a kilogram or two just by altering the amount of fluid she took in one day. At one point, her room had to be searched as she would hide a bottle of water under her bed or in her wardrobe, and quickly drink a litre of it before being weighed. A solution we came up with was to do random, unannounced weighs. She also used to try to hide things like a mobile phone or some other object in her underwear or clothing to affect the reading. Now she was only weighed in her underwear.

Another tactic was employed at dinnertime, when she would cut up the vegetables and meat, and move them around the plate to make it look like she had eaten something.

I was not given any patients that day. My job was to sit by Jeneil's bed and make sure she didn't get out and walk. I didn't speak to her and she didn't speak to me. Ignoring a patient was the opposite of what nurses do; it felt unnatural, but then again, there was nothing natural about this whole situation, and not speaking, in this case, was safer.

Just when it appeared things couldn't get any worse, they did. Jeneil began writhing around the bed. When she wasn't writhing, she was lifting her legs, or raising her head and chest, off the bed. She was exercising. With a sense of utter helplessness I rang the call bell. Mary entered the room and tried to reason with Jeneil.

Unfortunately, there was no reasoning with Jeneil. Her weight dropped to 40 kilograms and

223

she was transferred to the intensive care unit.

The psychiatric department had a meeting about Jeneil's transfer to the intensive care unit. All the nurses and all the doctors were there. We were not a specialist anorexia unit, and some suggested maybe Jeneil should have been in one, but she had already been in the best anorexia hospital in the country, multiple times, with no success.

Now 26, Jeneil had battled with anorexia from the age of 16, although it wasn't until she left high school that her weight loss had become so noticeable that her family sought medical intervention. She had no apparent reason for her condition. She came from a normal family, with a brother and sister who were healthy, and seemed happy. It just didn't make sense.

Jeneil died in the intensive care unit. Her heart gave out. Even if she had somehow been able to change, and had started eating and leading a healthy life, she would have had to live with permanent damage: her organs had suffered; her growth was stunted; her bones were brittle; and she would never have been able to have children.

Jeneil's death was tragic, but I'm not sure if it was avoidable. I'll never forget the head psychiatrist's words when news of Jeneil's death reached us: 'When they get to the stage Jeneil was at, it's almost always fatal.'

Catherine, meet your new neighbours

Our psychiatric unit was unusual in that we didn't have separate facilities for the very young, the very old or the very aggressive. It made for an interesting mix of people. For some patients, this was all they knew and nothing surprised them. For others, particularly those involved in the world inside their head, there wasn't much that could shock them. But there were some people whom you or I might consider normal — rational people who suddenly found themselves in the middle of this madhouse — for whom time in our ward was certainly an eye opening experience.

Catherine was 18 when she was brought to the psychiatric unit. She was polite and clever — due to graduate from high school in a few months' time. She had great grades, and had been accepted into university. She had a bright future in front of her. Until she did something that could potentially affect the rest of her life. She attempted to overdose on paracetamol.

Catherine needed help, and wanted people to know it. She thought by overdosing on a legal drug it would make people take her seriously.

Paracetamol is one of the safest yet also the most dangerous drugs in the world. Most people think it harmless, and why wouldn't they? It's often the first line of drugs given to children, even infants. It is safe, completely safe, in the right dosage.

What many people don't know is that if too much is taken, paracetamol destroys the liver. Even a moderate overdose — as little as a dozen tablets — can cause permanent damage. Higher doses can mean death, or at a minimum, the need for a new liver.

Fortunately for Catherine her liver had been saved. As soon as she had taken her overdose, she'd called an ambulance. When she'd been brought into the emergency room, the staff commenced an infusion of a drug which acts as an antidote to paracetamol.

I'd been working in the psychiatric unit for over a year when I met Catherine, and I was still considered inexperienced. I was rarely given female patients — instead, I was generally allocated younger males, sometimes aggressive. But today, as there was a shortage of young troubled male teenagers for me to look after, I was assigned Catherine.

Even though Catherine was technically an adult, she was still a school kid, and I knew it would be best to keep a close eye on her until she got used to the place.

I found Catherine walking down the corridor, clinging to the wall, unable to stop herself staring at everyone who passed. 'Why do they look like that?' she whispered to me as a particularly interesting specimen walked by.

'What do you mean?' I replied.

'You know what I mean, look at him,' she said.

The case in question was Jacob, a 35-year-old schizophrenic who'd been diagnosed at the age of 16. I knew Jacob well and I knew what Catherine was talking about, but I wanted to hear what she had to say — not out of spite, but so that she could get the most of her experience in a psychiatric unit.

'Well . . . ' She paused, thinking carefully about what she should say. 'He just looks insane. And what is he smiling at? It gives me the creeps.'

When Jacob's schizophrenia was in a good mood, the voices in his head were nice, sometimes even entertaining (although what you or I might find entertaining may not be exactly the same as what Jacob found entertaining), perhaps he was smiling at that. Of course, there was every possibility he was laughing at the cursing and other foul language directed at us, originating from the monster standing beside me.

Catherine and I made our way to the dining hall. I found her a table near the door, and left her alone while I rounded up the stragglers for dinner. I had just herded the last of the patients into the dining hall when I noticed Jeffrey sitting, staring at his food, mumbling under his breath.

Jeffrey was 20 years old, and like Jacob he suffered from schizophrenia. I'd slowly got to know Jeffrey over the few weeks since he had been admitted, and it had taken all that time before he began to acknowledge me. Well, acknowledge me probably isn't quite right, it took him that much time to begin to trust me.

Every day when I began work, I had to show him my staff ID card to prove that I was actually a nurse.

'Everything okay?' I asked. Jeffrey looked up from his plate, and mumbled an incoherent reply.

'What was that?'

'I'm not in the mood. Leave me alone.'

I left Jeffrey in peace, but stayed in the doorway observing the diners, as well as glancing regularly in his direction.

Jeffrey had done what some people with schizophrenia commonly do. He had stopped taking his medications. Sometimes the reason for this is that the medications they take make a huge difference. They can completely stop the voices or visions, and allow patients to lead a completely normal life. What then happens is the patient might start to think they are cured. Maybe they forget to take their medications regularly, maybe they're sick of the side effects of their prescription, or maybe they start drinking a bit of alcohol, or have a puff of a joint. In some cases all it takes is one smoke or one night out on the booze to hurl them back into an acutely schizophrenic state.

Jeffrey was studying architecture at university. He'd not had an admission to hospital in two years, mainly because he took his medications. He had then begun to occasionally forget his medications, before he stopped altogether.

Unfortunately, he didn't recognise that he was falling into a crisis. It was only after his mother got concerned that he wasn't answering his phone for several days that she paid him a visit and found him locked in his room, terrified of the world outside.

Paranoia is a common presentation. It can begin with something simple, like the voices start telling them that the medicine is really poisoned, but the delusions can come in an endless variety of ways. Maybe the television starts broadcasting straight into their heads. Whether it be a subtle, or sudden and violent, relapse, it is a very serious and frightening state to be in, both for the patient and the family or friends around them.

When I next glanced at Jeffrey, I noticed him staring intently at Mr Pike. Mr Pike was looking at the garden. He usually waited until everyone else had finished eating, then would sit and have his meal in peace and quiet. He was 45 years old, and had a history of bipolar disorder. He was due to be discharged soon.

Mr Pike hadn't noticed a thing. I kept watch, wondering what was going through Jeffrey's head. For five minutes his gaze didn't leave Mr Pike. I maintained my vigil.

Slowly, Jeffrey rose from his seat, and casually walked towards his subject. When he was an arm's length away, he lashed out and his fist caught Mr Pike across the cheek. I yelled out down the corridor for help as I stepped into the fray.

'I'll kill the little shit,' yelled Mr Pike. I was standing between the two, with arms outstretched, holding them apart. 'Why'd you fucking do it?' Jeffrey shouted back and lunged at Mr Pike. I managed to hold Jeffrey back. His gaze fell on me. 'Are you in it with him? You're in this together.'

It was at this point that I realised just how vulnerable I was. It dawned on me that I was standing between a furious Mr Pike and an obviously acutely psychotic Jeffrey.

'I'm sorry, Mr Pike, please don't hit him back. He's just a kid really. He's really unwell. We'll sort it out,' I rambled.

'He hit me. I'll kill the little shit,' Mr Pike said again.

'I can't let you do it. Let me talk to Jeff for one minute.'

'Why'd you hit him, Jeff?'

'He spat on my food.'

'Jeff, no one spat on your food. I was watching the whole time, and I promise you, no one spat on your food.'

Jeffrey paused in his efforts to reach Mr Pike and thought my words over.

'Jeff, you've trusted me before today. Remember, I see you each morning, and I show you my ID. You know you can trust me,' I pleaded. 'Just sit down, Jeff, please.' He didn't budge.

It felt like forever, but was probably only 30 seconds before the rest of the staff came rushing in, to find me standing with arms outstretched, holding back the antagonists.

'You're all in on it, you're all together,' Jeffrey said, before taking a swing at me. Before the blow could land, the ladies had Jeffrey immobilised.

Jeff was taken to seclusion and given a strong injection of medication to calm him down.

Throughout the whole affair, Catherine had sat open-mouthed, speechless and terrified. She stayed glued to me for the rest of the evening. 'What have I done?' she kept on saying to herself, to me, to anyone that would listen. 'I don't belong here.'

Psychiatric units like mine can be brutal at times, but they serve a purpose. For some patients, the psychiatric unit is a wake-up call. They realise just how lucky they are to be healthy and sane, with a future ahead of them.

Many of the patients here don't have a future. Sometimes, in their lucid moments, they realise this, and some lash out. But for the most part, the patients have no idea of how lost they are. Perhaps they just don't have time to think about it because their reality is already occupied with what's going on inside their head.

With counselling and the support of family and friends, Catherine made it back to school. Her overdose was deemed a cry for help, rather than a genuine attempt on her life. I do know she graduated and went to university. I never saw her again. I hope I never do.

As for young Jeffrey, it took three weeks to get him back on track. By the time he left, there was no way you would have ever guessed just how sick he had been. As long as he stays on his medications, he should hopefully be fine. He went back to university to finish his studies.

★ ★ ★

I spent two years working in the psychiatric unit before I was ready for a change. I wasn't bored with psychiatric nursing — how could I be? — but there was another area of nursing that I had always wanted to work in: the emergency room.

I felt ready for the challenge. The emergency room deals with everything, and I felt that my experiences overseas, combined with my broad experiences in various fields of nursing, especially with my recent ones in the psychiatric unit, would make me the perfect fit for it.

V

Family man of steel

Rangi Nelson was a freezing worker. If you are unsure what that is, it involves killing sheep, cattle and pigs for a living. The hours are long, with the slaughter going on through the night during high season. It is the sort of work that breeds strong men, both physically and mentally.

Rangi had been working the evening shift and was on his way home. It was ten o'clock at night, and he was tired. Thankfully, at that time, the back country roads are deserted. Rangi didn't have a car, or a motorbike, he had a 100cc moped — not what you might expect a tough meat worker to be riding, but he was trying to gather together enough money to put a deposit on his own home. He was sick of his family having to live in state housing.

The first 13 or so kilometres from the freezing works to the city were pretty much a straight line. The only hazard was a single pair of railway tracks crossing the road. The railway line was rarely busy — most people made only the most cursory of efforts to slow down. Aside from a sign with a picture of a train, there was no warning.

That night, Rangi was jolted out of his daze as a train came seemingly out of nowhere straight towards him. There's nothing like a thousand-tonne train, loaded with coal and wood, hurtling towards you at 100 kilometres an hour, to wake you up. He managed to stop just in time.

Suddenly Rangi found himself slammed into the side of the passing train. A car had come from behind and the driver had not seen Rangi on his little moped.

I was in the emergency room when Rangi came in.

I had only just transferred from the psychiatric unit two weeks earlier, and I was still being orientated to the emergency room. I was working alongside an experienced nurse called Shona, and I was only counted as an extra and not one of the rostered staff. Only after two months could I be considered a junior staff member.

In those two weeks, I had already learnt new skills and gained valuable experience, but there was one thing missing, one thing which I felt it very important that I be part of: a serious trauma.

All the experienced emergency room nurses had stories to tell about traumas, times when they had got their hands dirty; when they had battled against great odds and triumphed over death. To be a real emergency room nurse, I needed to experience a serious trauma, I needed to work alongside a team of pros, beat the odds to come out a battle-hardened veteran.

When the call came through telling us that the paramedics were bringing in a man who had been hit by a train, I just knew I had to be involved. I know how horrendous that sounds, ghoulish even, but this is the way many emergency room nurses are, they love the action, the challenge, they want to prove themselves to their peers. The nurse in charge could see how eager I was and gave me the all clear to begin preparing for the action.

My mind went blank.

I tried to remember what I was supposed to prepare, but it was hard to think where to begin: you don't often hear of people surviving being hit by a train. The only thing I knew was that it was going to be bad.

Fortunately, I remembered my ABC. As you might expect, ABC makes the basics simple. It helps you figure out what equipment you're going to need.

A is for **Airway** . . . But in this case, I didn't know if the patient was intubated, or breathing on his own. I eventually managed to think of something useful and began checking that the oxygen was flowing, and the suction working.

B is for **Breathing** . . . The patient might have a clear airway, but would he be breathing? And how well? Rapid and shallow? Slow and irregular? Would he be struggling? Would there be gurgling or other noises upon respiration?

I tried to imagine what sort of injury a train could do to a chest. A collapsed lung or pneumothorax seemed likely, which would hinder breathing. Technically a collapsed lung isn't really a collapse of the lung. What happens is the lung is made up of layers, and the outermost layer connects to the chest wall or ribcage. In cases of trauma, for example a stab wound to the chest, air from outside enters through the wound, filling up the space with trapped air. The air can get trapped between the layers that make up the skin of the lung. This then pushes against the rest of the lung, forcing it into a smaller and smaller space. So you need a drain that creates a one-way valve, allowing this trapped air out, and relieving the pressure.

I grabbed the equipment needed to insert a chest drain.

C is for **C**irculation . . . What would the patient's blood be doing? Leaking out on to the floor, or squirting up to the roof? Maybe there would be no obvious wounds, but the blood pressure might be extremely low, which could mean internal bleeding. In terms of preparation, this meant making sure we had the necessary equipment to provide intravenous access: intravenous catheters, central line. We also needed fluids and blood transfusions.

Thankfully I was not left to handle the preparations alone. While I had been running around like a headless chicken, the other staff had notified the surgeon and the anaesthetist and arranged all the things that I had missed.

This was shaping up to be harder than I'd thought.

As the ambulance pulled into the bay, the adrenaline began to flow. Looking around at the surgeon, the doctor, the anaesthetist, the radiographer and the other nurses, I could see the signs of a rush as well: nervous laughter at a bad joke, last minute checks of equipment that had already been checked ten times, slight tremors in a hand as someone tried to draw up some medicine. Everyone was ready for action.

As the doors crashed open and the paramedics

wheeled in the casualty we got our first sight of Rangi. Aside from the fact his head was strapped down and immobilised by a collar to protect his neck, there was no obvious injury to his face. He was awake and seemed to be breathing normally. This was always a good start. As we transferred him over to the trauma bed, the paramedics said he had a very severe leg injury but was otherwise okay.

All the same, the doctor began his inspection at the head. I knew this was what he was supposed to do, **ABC** again, but I wanted to have a look at that leg and I began to unfold the blanket that was being used as a bandage from around his left lower leg.

As I pulled the last blanket away from his injured left side, I let it drop to the floor. The leg was a mess — at least, what there was of it. There seemed to be a fair amount of the lower leg missing. I glanced down and was horrified to see quite a bit of it caught in the blanket I had dropped, along with plenty of blood and some shattered bones.

I didn't know what to do. The letters **ABC**, **ABC** kept going through my head, but it wasn't doing me any good. In a moment of madness, I considered brushing the blanket under the table as if nothing was the matter.

I was pretty sure Rangi wouldn't appreciate me asking him what he wanted done with the remains of his leg. I thought of wrapping it up and disposing of it in the rubbish bin, but the surgeons can do a pretty amazing job at times, so it was worth keeping all the pieces and hoping they could put his leg back together.

It is moments like these that nothing can really prepare you for. There is no class at college that tells you what to do when you drop a patient's leg on the floor; no acronym. The doctor suggested I wrap everything up and put it to the side for the moment. He then wisely suggested I get some more morphine.

Rangi was wide awake the whole time; he was even talking to the doctors and nurses as he was stuck with all manner of frightening looking instruments. I will never forget his reaction when the doctor explained what had happened to his leg. He was told that they could try to piece his leg back together, but there would be little point, he would lose it in the end.

Maybe it was the shock, but Rangi calmly replied, 'Do what you have to do.'

Rangi was rushed to the operating theatre where they amputated the lower part of his leg. His life was changed forever. Even though I never saw him again, I do know he was eventually discharged from the surgical ward, to the rehabilitation ward, and then home.

Rangi could no longer work as a freezing worker, at least not in the near future, but he still had to support his family. New Zealand has a system where we can't sue each other for damages. The driver who caused the damage would have gone to court and possibly faced a jail sentence, but could not have compensated the victim financially. Thankfully, New Zealand has an accident compensation system where the government provides money, as well as pays for the things needed to help Rangi gain his independence again. They can even provide money for retraining in a new job if needed.

As for me, I learnt two things that day. One: don't be so eager to be in the thick of it, and two: even after half a dozen years of nursing, I still had a lot to learn.

Dumb as they come

I rapidly came to realise that human stupidity is acutely highlighted in the emergency room.

For anyone who is unaware of how brainless people can be, just come and spend a day at your local hospital. I remember one man who was seen four times for the same type of injury. Once is acceptable, twice is stupid, three times is suicidal, and four is unbelievable. The silly idiot was not wearing eye protection when welding. His eyes were so red, I thought he was going to cry blood, which would have been a first for me. The pain must have been unbearable. Every time he was led from the department by his wife, he promised he would wear eye protection. But evidently severe pain and the risk of going blind is not a good enough incentive to use common sense.

It is even more common to see people in the hospital because they haven't worn their seatbelt. It's amazing the damage a windscreen can do to a face if you happen to go through it head first. If you somehow manage to avoid fracturing your skull, then the hundreds of lacerations make for quite an impressive sight.

For one particular young man, only 21 years of age, who crashed his car on a quiet country road, I could almost understand why he didn't bother putting on his seatbelt: it was five in the morning, he was on his way to milk his cows, and the milking sheds were only one kilometre down the road. The last thing he expected was to encounter another car. But one morning he did, and a miracle occurred: he survived going headfirst through the windscreen.

'I think I need some fresh air,' Amber said, racing for the door.

Like myself, Amber was a young nurse, new to the emergency room; this was her first trauma. I kept my face expressionless, a sign of a truly hardened emergency room nurse — at least that was how I hoped I looked. The patient in front of me certainly did not look *his* best. His skull was intact, but his face was a mass of lacerations; loose flesh dangled from his cheeks, chin and forehead. It was as if someone high on speed had taken a cheese grater and gone to work. The worst thing of all was that his forehead was missing. The skin had been peeled back like an onion, and sat in a line of ridges across the centre of his head, running from ear to ear. It was no surprise that Amber needed some fresh air.

'What's your name?' I asked the young man.

All I got back were some incomprehensible sounds — bubbling and gurgling noises.

'Sorry, can you say it again?' I repeated as I leant closer to hear more clearly.

Every time he opened his mouth or tried to breathe through his nose, the blood kept on forming bubbles, but I finally deciphered a name: Darren. He spat out two of his teeth as he said this. I calmly picked them up and put them in a clean urine specimen bottle and then put

243

them in a property bag. I didn't bother getting him to sign the property form.

Despite not wearing his seatbelt, Darren was thankfully alive and by the looks of things he had no life threatening injuries. Okay, his face was rearranged, but he was breathing fine, although his broken teeth were proving to be a bit of a nuisance. He had no broken bones and no sign of organ damage or haemorrhaging, and the most unbelievable thing of all was that Darren insisted that he had been conscious the whole time.

Darren went from the emergency room straight to the operating theatre. He was operated on for three hours, until eventually being admitted into a general surgical ward. I came to work the next day, a Monday which was also a public holiday. It was eerily quiet in the emergency room, which was strange — Monday was usually one of our busiest days. (It's amazing how people don't get sick on public holidays.) It was so quiet, I was asked to lend a hand in the general surgical ward and it was here that I bumped into Darren again.

What a sight he was; he had over two dozen different suture lines zigzagging all over his face but my eyes were drawn to the massive zip that was tattooed across his forehead just above his eyebrows. He looked like something out of a Frankenstein movie; his face was literally being held together by a thread. There was still a lot of dried crusty blood and bits of glass in his hair and on his face. He looked miserable, but when he saw me walk in the door he gave me a big

244

gap-toothed smile. I felt sure that his smile would fade once he saw himself in the mirror.

I really wanted to do something to clean him up a bit. I started with some of the small fragments of glass that were still peppered over his face and in his hair, and then moved on to the dried blood.

As I carefully and gently began to remove the dried blood from his face, his cheerful demeanour began to slip away.

'Shit that hurts. Is there an easier way to do this?' asked Darren as I began pulling at a particularly sticky globule of dried blood. 'Are you sure you know what you are doing?'

'Of course, don't worry, you will feel much better once I've finished,' I reassured him.

I became totally engrossed in the job — I might even go so far as to describe it as quite enjoyable, relaxing work — and soon I began looking for other ways to clean things up.

There were lots of long pieces of suture material all over his face. Some were dangling in front of his eyes, and he kept on having to brush them away, and some were stuck to his face in thick globules of dried blood. I trimmed some of the longer bits of spare suture material, and tried pulling some of the strings of suture free from the lumps of blood they were stuck in. I pulled too hard . . .

'Oops . . . bugger . . . No nothing, Darren. I didn't swear. No seriously, everything is okay.'

I couldn't believe how dumb I had just been. In my eagerness to clean him up, the right cheek had been pulled very slightly downwards; his right cheek was the tiniest bit lower than the left. I was in big trouble and the surgeon wouldn't be happy, if he found out.

Sometimes the stupidest things are done with the best of intentions — I pictured the right side of Darren's face peeling off. I kept a smile on my face and my breathing even. I did not want Darren to worry. I felt sure I could fix it. The only thing I could think of was to give it a pull the other way. I took the other end of the suture and gently pulled. To my immense relief his right cheek moved up and back into alignment.

'I think that's enough cleaning for today, Darren.'

The next day I woke and during breakfast managed to have a quick glance at the paper. Staring at me from the front page was a picture of Darren with that gap-toothed smile. I felt like I had been hit in the chest — Darren must have complained about me, or told a friend or family member that I had been messing with his face.

I began to read the article with trepidation, certain that my nursing days were over, but I soon realised with relief that I wasn't in trouble. Darren was being used as a promotion for the land transport safety authority. His mangled face was a warning for all of us to buckle up. Darren was actually happy having his image on the front page. The article stated that Darren hadn't been wearing his seatbelt, but now he had learnt his lesson and would always wear it from now on.

I thought I had seen the last of Darren, but that was not to be.

Two months later, Darren appeared in the

newspaper again. He had been pulled over and given a fine by a police officer for not wearing his seatbelt. He was on his way to milk his cows, on the very same stretch of road where he'd had the accident.

Don't believe all you read

I sometimes wonder if the shocking picture of Darren's face on the front page of the newspaper saved any lives. Even if it didn't, it was a nice gesture. Unfortunately, from my experience, newspapers are rarely nice to hospitals, or the people that work in them. I can only assume that papers print what people want to read, which is something shocking, something to really make people get emotional about. It doesn't seem to necessarily matter what emotion that is, but anger and shock always seem to draw people in.

I remember very clearly one story where the newspaper got it utterly wrong. It wasn't a big fat lie, just a slight error in reporting all the facts. But it only takes a slight error, or a failure to present all the information, to make a big impact.

One of the most challenging aspects of emergency medicine is triage. Triage simply means deciding what needs to be seen first. The most life threatening will get seen immediately, while the less urgent will have to wait. It may sound simple, but it's not. A typical example of where it gets difficult is someone presenting with a simple fever. By itself, this is pretty harmless, but what if it's the early stages of a serious illness; an illness that can kill in a matter of hours?

When Mr and Mrs Goodwin presented to the

front desk, I was the one doing the triaging. Cradled in Mrs Goodwin's arms was a young boy, naked, except for a nappy, and covered in a blanket. He looked about 18 months old. As soon as I saw the baby, alarm bells immediately began to ring.

'He was okay this morning. He only became really sick at dinnertime. I've never seen him like this.'

As Mrs Goodwin gave a history, I began checking the baby's temperature, respiration rate, and body for signs of a rash. He had a high fever, but what was more worrying was how quiet the child was.

'Has he had a cough, blocked nose or any other symptoms?' Both parents said that their son had previously been well.

'He was a bit off colour this morning, off his food, a bit flushed. I just thought it was a normal virus, but he's so hot, and so quiet. He was fine yesterday, running around playing happily,' explained Mrs Goodwin.

It's not unusual to have unexplained fever in children. It's easy to blame it on some passing virus. But when you can't find the cause, you can't rule out something more serious. Even if you can find a probable cause, like a common cold, you still can't rule out something more dangerous.

From my brief encounters with children in hospital, I had learnt that, even when sick, they are often still full of energy. It's when they stop playing, stop even crying, that you know you need to worry. This is because they may have reached a critical stage of their illness. I spent only five minutes examining the Goodwins' child, before taking him straight through to the emergency room to see the doctor.

Dr Munroe was the junior doctor working that day, and when I explained my concerns, he saw the child straight away. After a quick examination, blood and urine samples were taken and an intravenous line inserted.

The urine test took two minutes, and came back clear; but the initial blood test, which came back shortly after, indicated an infection. The problem was, no one knew what sort of infection. It was at this stage that Dr Munroe sought the advice of his senior, Dr Jackson.

The fear we all had was that the child might have meningitis. This infamous disease can present as a simple viral illness, but then kill within 24 hours. The only way to confirm the infection is to insert a needle between the vertebrae and take a sample of the spinal fluid. This takes time. The decision that needed to be made was whether to commence the child on antibiotics straight away.

Dr Jackson had dealt with many cases like this, and he took the prudent course of action, and commenced intravenous antibiotics immediately. He explained to the family that their child would still need a spinal tap, or lumbar puncture, at some stage, but that this wasn't so urgent now that treatment was started.

'Why does he still need a spinal tap, if you're treating him for meningitis anyway?' Mrs Goodwin asked. She understandably wasn't keen on her child having the procedure. It's unpleasant, particularly for a child, as you have to have several staff members holding the child still while the doctor inserts the needle. The child screams, and tries to wriggle free, but you just have to hold them firm, and not let them move.

'We have to know for sure what is making your child so sick,' explained Dr Jackson. 'We're treating him for the worst case scenario, but we don't know for sure. We can't base our treatment on assumptions. We don't want to miss anything else.' Dr Jackson also explained that if it was bacterial meningitis, the rest of the family would need a course of antibiotics as well.

'I don't want to be there when they do it.' Mrs Goodwin turned to her husband. 'You'll have to be there for me. I won't be able to bear it.' Mr Goodwin held his wife for a moment, before turning to Dr Jackson.

Fortunately the spinal tap was going to be done in the children's ward. Less fortunately, there were no beds free at that time. Mr and Mrs Goodwin had a three-hour wait in the emergency room before a bed became available and they were transferred to the care of a specialist paediatric doctor.

Once in the children's ward, a spinal tap confirmed the diagnosis of bacterial meningitis. We'd done the right thing by starting treatment straight away. We'd saved another life.

It was several days after my dealings with the Goodwin family that I saw them again. They were on the front page of the local newspaper. It reported that a young child with meningitis had to wait three hours to see a doctor. Sure, there had been a wait to see a specialist doctor, and be admitted to the ward. But there was no mention made of me or the two doctors who initially treated their child.

I can only guess that the parents wanted something more from the hospital, but what more did they want than us saving their child's life?

I no longer believe any medical story I read in the newspaper, no matter how realistic it may seem, as I've seen them get it very wrong on several occasions. It's frustrating that the hospital often doesn't respond, as they can't break patient confidentiality. It seems a double standard to me — the patient or family are often only too happy for the world to hear of their time in hospital, so why can't we return the favour? I wonder if that would cut the number of complaints.

Unfortunately, nurses and doctors can't afford to make mistakes as we're meant to be immaculate, but in reality we're simply human. With the numbers of people coming to emergency rooms increasing, along with the variety of treatments on offer, statistically, there will be errors.

Confidential dilemmas

Most people will have heard of the Hippocratic Oath at some time or another. Issues of ethics and medicine are pretty tightly bound together, wherever you are. I have encountered similar moral dilemmas in both New Zealand and the UK, particularly when it comes down to the right to confidentiality. Sometimes it can be rather riling that medical staff cannot discuss patients, but they are free to discuss us. But then again, everyone needs to have someone they can turn to in complete privacy, when they may have no one else, and I'm happy to be able to be that person.

Things are rarely black and white, take these occasions for example:

1. I remember one woman who had tripped over some steps as she left the pub, and needed sutures for a cut on her face. She had driven herself, drunk, to the emergency room. Once she'd been treated, I offered to ring for a taxi to take her home. She refused. I even offered for the hospital to pay for the transport. She refused. Instead, she got into her car, still drunk. My colleagues claim that technically I broke the law when I phoned the police. Thankfully, the woman didn't make it out of the hospital driveway because she crashed into the barrier at the hospital entrance. She

wasn't hurt, though I was more worried about others she may have hurt. She was arrested.

2. Another time, a 15-year-old girl came in following an accidental drug overdose. She was about one month pregnant and had tried to abort the foetus using a combination of emergency contraceptive tablets, ibuprofen and alcohol. She had not gone to a medical professional because she feared they'd tell her parents. The law in New Zealand states we cannot divulge sexual health to parents without the child's consent. As much as I think it's generally a good idea to involve a minor's parents, and might encourage it, there are exceptions, and I'm grateful for this rule: often kids need someone and some-where safe they can turn to — especially if this prevents them from taking matters into their own hands.

3. Probably the most unusual instance occurred at my local pub, when I lived in New Zealand. I was out with some friends when a very attractive woman approached us, and offered to buy me a drink. It took me a moment to recognise her. The last time I'd seen her she looked pretty terrible. I politely refused. My friends then wanted me to introduce them to her.

   The woman in question had been a psychiatric patient in my care. She was a very unstable schizophrenic and spent the majority of her life in and out of the psychiatric unit. This was a real tough one for me. I strongly believed in her right to be treated like a normal person, and in this respect, I should have let my friends chat her up. But at the same time, she was a genuinely troubled soul and I couldn't let a friend walk blind into a complicated situation. In some of her lucid moments, I'd heard her refer to her psychiatric medications as rape drugs. Ultimately, I refused, and my friends were pissed. But I left the pub and my friends followed me, none of them any the wiser.

The perfect match

Nursing boards in both New Zealand and the UK insist that we spend so many hours each year updating our skills. This generally includes things like basic CPR and correct lifting practice, as well as anything else that a nurse is particularly interested in. These hours can be fulfilled on an individual basis, or sometimes hospitals put on special conferences where guest speakers come to speak to the assembled nurses.

I hate to say it, but as a rule these mass education sessions can be a bit boring, particularly when you're learning about things you already know. But for me there is one major exception, which is when we're discussing ethical issues like confidentiality. As challenging and complex as these sorts of issues can be to deal with in real life, in the classroom, I enjoy them. I've always enjoyed a good debate — although my wife would say 'argument'.

On one particular occasion, as part of our ongoing education, I was one of about a hundred nurses receiving a lecture on patient care ethics. The union rep caused quite a stir. She said that 'Nurses should be discouraged from marrying their patients.' There was a loud murmur of disapproval around the room, which surprised me. I didn't think this was such a big deal. In fact, I assumed that most nurses would realise this, but I guessed from comments I overheard

— which ranged from 'That's bullshit' to 'Who the fuck do they think they are?' — that more of my colleagues than I'd imagined had married people they'd looked after.

The speaker also seemed surprised by the hum of displeasure, and although she didn't back-pedal, she did become slightly more conciliatory: 'Well, of course, we can't stop you, and, of course, nothing would happen regarding your registration, but we do recommend that you do not enter into relationships with your patients.'

The rep then asked for a show of hands of nurses who had married patients. I got quite a surprise when I saw that nearly a third of nurses put up their hands.

To be honest, I think this is fine. Hell, most male patients, of all ages, flirt with the nurses. So I've seen many of them make the first tentative moves.

On the other hand, things are a little different when the nurse is a male. Friendly as I endeavour to be, I would not want to be seen to be genuinely flirting with a patient. Nor have I often experienced female patients making the first moves on me.

That said, sometimes it's different outside of the hospital. I was at a bar one Friday night when a woman came up to me and with no warning, kissed me on the lips. She was very attractive and I naturally responded.

'You don't remember me, do you?' she finally said when our lips parted.

I was racking my brain, desperately trying to recall who she was. My future sex life might depend on me remembering where I'd met this woman before.

She just smiled. 'Don't worry, I've changed a lot. You looked after me when I had my surgery. I just wanted to say thank you for being such a great nurse.'

I suddenly remembered who she was. Not her name, damn it, but at least the circumstances. She had had Crohn's disease (inflammation of the bowel) and had needed an operation. She was obviously doing well as she'd put on some healthy weight, and looked positively gorgeous . . . My hopes remained high. Until: 'I have to go, my boyfriend will be here soon, but I just had to say thank you.' She gave me another kiss on the lips, then disappeared into the night.

That's about as close as I ever came.

No chance

About a year into my time in the emergency room, I began to feel competent — if competent meant knowing when and where to get help. Every day was a learning curve, and if it wasn't a new disease or a bizarre accident that kept me on my toes, then it was something psychological or emotional.

The hospital environment is a place where we meet the good, the bad and the just plain messed up. On any given day you will see the wealthy sick, the poor sick, the rude sick and the bad sick. And then there are the children. Infants are my one true weakness, I turn into a bumbling, useless idiot; they are so small, so fragile, so completely dependent on you.

It was three o'clock on a Friday afternoon the day I met baby Alice. Things were just starting to get busy; it was only a matter of time before the usual Friday night alcohol-related injuries began trickling in: assaults, car accidents, comatose intoxicated.

BEEEEEEEP!

I still always jumped when the blue phone rang. It was so loud, the whole department could hear it. It wouldn't have surprised me if one day it gave a patient a heart attack. The blue phone is the phone used by paramedics to give us advance warning of a particularly sick patient that's coming in. So, as ever, I picked it up expecting the worst.

'Ambulance 13 to hospital; do you read me? Over.'

'Hospital receiving; go ahead, ambulance 13,' I replied.

'We have on board a 27-year-old woman and a three-month-old infant. Please have security waiting when we arrive.'

I was a bit surprised; they would usually say what was actually wrong with the patients; they didn't even say which, or both, needed to be seen. That got the alarm bells ringing. Why didn't they tell us anything? It probably meant that the mother was causing trouble.

I went to stand in the ambulance bay beside the hospital security guard, Jamie, the world's *smallest* security guard. It's a strange phenomenon, but most hospital security guards I've met tend to be either a bit undersized or look near retirement age.

'Give me back my baby, you bastard.'

The woman wasn't even in through the hospital doors yet, but she could be heard by everyone.

'She's my baby, fuck you. Fuck you all! Give her fucking back.'

The woman made a grab for her child, but tripped over her own feet, landing on the ground with an audible thump.

I'm not picking her up, was the first thought that went through my head. I didn't move from my spot but glanced down at Jamie.

'Looks like you've got your hands full there, Jamie. Don't take any crap from her,' I said.

Jamie, a veteran, had dealt with situations like this before and prudently made a call to the police.

I then saw Alice, she was cradled in the arms of Tim, our gentle-giant of a paramedic. Alice was beyond tiny; she was the littlest human being that I can remember seeing. She was gorgeous, even while crying at the top of her lungs.

'She hasn't stopped howling since I've had her,' said Tim, as he handed baby Alice to me.

Even howling didn't feel like a good enough word. This was a scream, a high-pitched wailing noise that sent shivers down my spine.

Tim must have read my mind. 'I've never heard a scream like it. It gives me goosebumps.'

As I carried Alice through to the treatment room, I briefly ran my eyes over her. I could see no sign of obvious injury. There were no deformed limbs, no bruises, lacerations, not even any bleeding. But that scream was triggering a memory deep down inside of me. I couldn't quite place my finger on it yet, but I knew it was something important.

'We were called to the supermarket at 1400 hours by the manager of the store,' Tim explained. 'Mrs Lawrence was on the escalator. Witnesses say she tripped and landed on top of her baby.'

The more Tim said, the more rapidly the memory found its way up from the depths.

'Mrs Lawrence claims she has only had a few drinks but as you can see she is very intoxicated. She was refusing to come to hospital to get Alice checked out but soon changed her mind when I threatened to call the police.'

At that moment the memory surfaced and I knew, without a doubt, what was wrong with Alice.

I glanced back out into the ambulance bay, to see Jamie picking Mrs Lawrence up off the concrete.

'Get your fucking hands off me, you bastard.'

Mrs Lawrence wasn't letting up with her verbal assault.

She was heading towards Tim and me, all the time continuing with a non-stop barrage of abuse that would make the most weather-beaten sailor blanch. By this time, Jamie had the help of two of my colleagues and, between the three of them, they herded Mrs Lawrence into a side room.

'I swear if she comes near me I'll lose it,' I told Tim.

I gently laid Alice down on the bed. That was a mistake. Just when I thought I had heard the worst that baby Alice's lungs had to offer, her screams jumped up several octaves, so I quickly picked her back up and with Alice held close I carefully made my way next door to find the consultant on duty.

Dr Nelson wasn't exactly a consultant; he never got around to sitting his final exams, but he was the backbone of our department. After 20 years of service, he had seen it all.

'I think you've got a sick one there,' he remarked calmly to me. 'Let's have a look, shall we.'

I wished I was as calm as Dr Nelson, instead I blurted out the obvious, 'The screaming is really bad, doc; it gets even worse when I lie her down.'

I didn't want to appear like a drama queen, and I didn't want to sound stupid if my diagnosis was wrong, but I had to speak my mind. One of my nursing tutors had told me about a special type of cry a baby makes, a cry that sets your teeth on edge. She had no other words to describe it, but she'd said we'd know it when we heard it.

'I'm worried she has a fractured skull.'

Dr Nelson calmly began to examine the baby.

'I think you're right, well done for bringing her to me straight away.'

The plan of action was to arrange a head CT as soon as possible. This is a pretty serious test to carry out on an infant, not only does it expose the baby's brain to potentially damaging X-rays, but you can't ask a baby to keep still, so they need to be put to sleep, and putting an infant to sleep with a head injury is really a big deal.

As we made arrangements with the anaesthetic consultant and his registrar, we heard a male voice bellow from reception: 'Where's my fucking baby? I want to see my baby now.'

Judging from the language being used I guessed this must be Dad. The poor receptionist didn't get a chance to respond as Dad came charging into the department. I really shouldn't judge people by appearances, but I've found in the emergency room that often first impressions are worth something. Dad was skinny, pale, goateed, tattooed and shaven-headed. He was also drunk. He reeked of heavy spirits and was at least as intoxicated as his wife.

'I'm sorry, Jay. I'm so fucking sorry, so sorry,' sobbed Mrs Lawrence, as she ran in, trailed by Jamie. 'They won't let me see her. The fucking arseholes won't let me near her.'

'Get them out of here now,' Dr Nelson said in the kind of tone that makes people bolt into action.

Jamie took hold of Mrs Lawrence.

'Get your hands off my fucking wife, you little bastard,' yelled Jay.

Thankfully, Tim the paramedic was still there, and moved to physically remove Jay from the department.

'I'll fucking sue the lot of you,' Jay said as he was led away. But he wasn't resisting; he was sensible enough not to push his luck any further. He tried a new tactic; one which I have seen many times.

'Look, I'm really sorry, guys. I'm just worried about my baby. Please, I'm really sorry.' He knew he had gone too far, realised he could end up being led away in handcuffs, and now he was trying the oh-so-caring-dad routine. 'Please, just tell me what is going on.'

'Your daughter is seriously unwell, Mr Lawrence. It looks like she has a fractured skull. She will be put to sleep and a scan will be done of her head,' Dr Nelson said. 'Depending on the scan, there is a possibility she will be transferred to another hospital in another city, where they have a specialist intensive care unit for infants.'

When Dr Nelson talked everyone listened, it

was those years of experience and the accumulation of knowledge filtering through every word he said. I actually thought he was getting through to Mr Lawrence.

'What did my wife do?'

Dr Nelson told him the full story — and Mr Lawrence turned his rage on to his wife.

She was standing in the doorway of her cubicle with the door half closed, ready to slam it shut if her husband made a sudden move towards her.

'Not your fucking fault!' Mr Lawrence said incredulously as Mrs Lawrence attempted to defend herself. 'You got pissed and fell on my baby. How the fuck isn't it your fault?'

'If you spent any time at home, you'd know just how it's your fault. Instead you're always at the pub, pissed.'

Mrs Lawrence looked directly at me.

'Do you know he can't get a job? We have no money and he pisses it all away. I married a fucking loser.'

Before we had time to react, Mr Lawrence charged towards his wife. She tried to slam the door shut, but he easily forced it open. In the seconds it took us to catch him, Mr Lawrence managed to deliver two hard fists to his wife's face. After making sure she was going to be okay, Mrs Lawrence went home with a social worker and Mr Lawrence went away in handcuffs after all.

Baby Alice did have a skull fracture but that was the last I saw of her; she was wheeled into the intensive care unit, to await transport to another hospital, in another city.

It wasn't until three months later that I eventually heard that she had made a full recovery. I also discovered she was back with her parents. This is sometimes the most frustrating part of the job, knowing that you can only fix a small (sometimes temporary) part of an often greater problem. All I can do is have faith that the powers that make this sort of decision are making the best choice for the child.

Saturday night shift

I worked for two years in the emergency room before I was considered one of the experienced staff members. No one ever said 'Hey, you're now an experienced staff member', but certain things began to happen. The most obvious change being that I found myself working more night shifts. The weekend night shift is always the most interesting . . .

There was a commotion at the security doors. The guard rushed over and asked for help. Several of us raced to the door to find a young man being carried by a group of very angry looking people.

The young man couldn't have been more drenched in blood if he had taken a bath in it. I have seen a fair amount of bleeding in my time, but rarely so much from one person — and never from one who was still alive.

I knew immediately who this must be. We'd had a call about ten minutes earlier from the paramedics asking if we'd had any stab victims. They'd been called to a party that was the scene of an alleged assault, but there was no victim, or witnesses. There was, however, a lot of blood, so much that they were worried somebody was seriously injured.

The young man on the other side of the security doors urgently needed our help, but there was one slight problem. We had to somehow get the victim inside to be treated, but keep the horde out, because there was no way we wanted them in the building. There must have been 20 people clamouring at the front door, yelling, angry, and probably drunk; far too many to control. With so few of us, they could easily have run riot and we would have been powerless to stop them.

This was not just about their numbers or aggression, our emergency department had a policy of no more than one family member in the resuscitation room, and they had introduced this policy for good reason. In my two years in the emergency room I'd seen and heard of plenty of incidences of violence and verbal abuse to treating staff.

In this particular case, the reasoning was even simpler; the paramedics had phoned from the scene of a party. Parties mean alcohol, and alcohol can bring out the worst in people.

As I've mentioned, Jamie, our security guard, wasn't exactly intimidating. There was no way he would be able to stop the crowd from coming inside. He'd just put himself at risk trying.

'Just stay out of their way,' I told Jamie. 'Stay in the background. The uniform might make you a target. You don't want to be mistaken for a cop.'

When people are angry, police officers can often find themselves targets. Jamie was more than happy to oblige.

We eventually opened the doors and I was almost knocked over by the inrush of bodies.

'*Fuck, do something! Fuck, you're a fucking*

doctor, *do something.*'

Everyone was shouting and screaming at once; the only words I could hear clearly were curses. It was chaos.

I returned my attention to the victim. So far he had not shown any sign of life.

I acted on instinct alone, and grabbed on to the body. It gave me a purpose and it gave me something to focus on. The other two nurses took hold of him as well, battling with two people, who turned out to be the boy's parents, who were not going to let go of their son.

Between the parents, me, and the two other nurses on duty that night, we managed to drag the patient past a stunned looking elderly man and on to the next resuscitation bed. The crowd of people followed us through.

I tried to explain that only two relatives could be here, but I was ignored, and decided it best not to argue.

The victim was a teenage boy. He was cold to touch and very pale. He looked as if he had been drained of all blood. There was certainly enough blood on his clothes and those around him, plus there was a trail leading out past reception to the front door. At that moment I began to worry about my own safety. I looked at my colleagues and I could tell they were thinking the same thing as me. The only help this boy could get was from a power greater than any we had to offer; he was dead.

But try telling the family there was nothing we could do. It was not an option, we had to at least make an effort, be seen to do something.

At my hospital, there was generally only one doctor on duty during the night. This was very often a junior doctor, but thankfully that evening we had Keith, an experienced practitioner with a full year of emergency room service behind him.

He jumped in with his first instructions: 'Start compressions. I'll try to get a line.'

It's a bit hard to find a vein on a corpse, so Keith stuck the needle in a vein in the side of the boy's neck. I began compressions, all the time trying to keep my fingers out of the chest wound. The stab wound was to the left side of the chest, directly into the right ventricle of the boy's heart, which explained the extent of the bleeding. With every beat of this boy's heart, his life had drained out of him. I tried to tune out slurping sounds coming from the wound every time I pressed down.

We continued resuscitation, knowing it was going to do no good. We poured in fluids, we poured in blood, and pumped him full of adrenaline, but it was to no avail. By this time three more nurses had come from other wards to help out. They had to fight their way through the crowd of onlookers just to get to the bedside.

'He's not moving. Fucking *do* something,' screamed a giant of a man who had nearly bowled me over earlier. When Keith suggested that resuscitation should be stopped, the boy's father responded immediately: 'You do and you fucking die!' He backed up his threat by pulling out a knife and brandishing it at Keith, and then me.

Keith signalled us to keep on going, even

though it was well past the point of no return.

Meanwhile, out at reception, another relative of the boy was standing in front of Joanne our receptionist, painting his face. Joanne didn't say a word as the man stuck his finger in a pool of blood and smeared it over his face. He was of Maori descent, and probably painting traditional war patterns on his face, getting ready for battle.

The receptionist didn't have the courage to tell the man that the blood was not from the stabbing victim, but from another patient.

Thankfully, all emergency rooms I've ever worked in have silent alarms that can be discreetly pressed. Joanne had pressed our emergency alarm the moment the family had arrived.

It felt like hours before the police came; in reality it was only 20 minutes. When you're in a crisis situation time changes; five minutes can seem like an eternity, or an hour can fly by and only feel like five minutes.

Half a dozen cars crammed full of officers pulled into the car park; it looked like the whole of the town's force was here. Usually the more junior police officers ended up dealing with hospital problems, but when they came into the resuscitation room there were older, obviously senior police officers that I had never seen before.

I'd never been so relieved to see the police as I was then. It turned out they were so delayed getting here because they had all gone to the scene of the stabbing, which was at the other end of town. Thankfully our town was small enough

271

for a stabbing to still be a big deal.

The police did a good job; they kept calm, ignored the abuse hurled at them and slowly managed to herd the crowd out of the department, with surprisingly (and thankfully) little hassle.

At that moment, resuscitation was stopped. All those who had taken turns jumping up and down doing compressions were particularly relieved; it's tiring work. The boy was taken to the morgue and we never saw the family again. Everyone was physically and emotionally drained, but, of course, there was no time to rest, as there were more patients still to see.

There had been one other man in resus when the commotion broke out. It was 86-year-old Mr Ripley, a regular patient who came in when his breathing got bad. He and his wife had been witness to the whole scenario. I didn't know what to say; perhaps I should've told him that this was not a typical Saturday night.

Mr Ripley was a veteran of the Second World War. He and his wife had been vulnerable. In all the mayhem I had forgotten about them. I cannot imagine what it would be like to face an enemy on the battlefield, but he had every reason to be as frightened as I was this night, as he sat there helpless, frail and ill, watching the madness, with no way to escape, with his wife sitting beside him. He was of course terrified for her, too.

He made a remark which I'll never forget: 'I've survived the war; seen my comrades die around me; charged machine guns; but I've never been as frightened as I was tonight.'

I never found out the full or true story of what happened that night, just what I read in the newspaper. It began as a family party with a few close friends. The victim had had a disagreement over a real or imagined insult about a girlfriend. The murderer was a teenage friend, who is now spending his days behind bars. The father ended up in court, although I never found out what the outcome was.

Security was increased after that incident, which meant two security guards instead of one.

As for me, well, I did just have a knife waved in my direction, but it was a busy Saturday night; there was no talk of time off or counselling. I kept on working, along with everyone else.

Full moon

The previous two nights had been the busiest I'd seen in the whole year. We had a record amount of drunken teenagers, a worrying number of assaults, six overdoses and five GDGAPWs, which stands for: got drunk, got angry, punched wall. The W can also be substituted for window.

As I pulled into work on the third evening, I wasn't greeted with the most encouraging of sights. Four ambulances were fighting to offload their burden and two police cars took up the last of the parking spaces; I felt like turning around. To make matters worse, there was a full moon in the sky. If I had noticed that before I had left home, I might have been tempted to call in sick. It was going to be a very interesting night.

'Evening all; looks like the madmen will be out in full force tonight,' I said by way of greeting.

'Too late, they're out already,' said Trish.

Trish had been on with me for the last two nights. She looked tired, and was showing the typical signs of someone at the end of a six-night run. She was a touch more cynical, a tad more sarcastic, and a wee bit short tempered. She was the lucky one, because I still had another two nights in front of me. My other partner in crime that night was

Amber. This was Amber's first time on night shift.

She smiled appropriately at our comments, as any new junior member of staff should, but I could tell she was not a believer.

'It's true, the full moon really does affect people,' I added. 'By the time the night is through you will see for yourself.'

I've never found any scientific evidence to substantiate the belief that the full moon affects people, but I have heard that some places provide an extra nurse when it's a full moon. I've even heard of some police departments deploying more officers.

My first patient for the evening was Mr Jones, one of our frequent flyers. His complaint was always the same: chest pain.

For some reason, Mr Jones's chest pain got miraculously better every time the paramedics wheeled him through the front door.

It's quite possible Mr Jones never had much chest pain to begin with. That type of patient isn't an unusual sight; there are many people in the community who are just in need of some company or reassurance.

Before I could begin assessing Mr Jones, we heard raised voices and cursing. It was coming from next door in minor injuries.

'Fuck the lot of ya' — it was a woman's voice — 'you're all bloody useless.'

I didn't want to investigate, but I made my way next door to see if anyone needed a hand. I walked in to find Amber trying to calm down an irate giant of a woman. She must have been six foot three inches tall, at least, and I estimated she weighed at least 130 kilograms. She had covered her flesh in a fluffy nightgown; it was pink with a white trim, and decorated with flowers.

'What're you staring at, ya little pervert?' she asked.

'This is Miss Turner. She won't wait to be seen,' Amber explained.

'I'm bloody sick and nobody believes me.'

The woman stank of beer and spirits. She wasn't sick; she was drunk.

'We believe you, we believe you,' said Amber, trying her best to placate the giant, 'but there are others sicker than you. You're going to have to wait.'

The woman conceded and sat back down on the bed.

'I'll leave you to it, Amber. Give me a yell if you need a hand,' I said and headed back next door.

'You can't please them all,' said Mr Jones, as I prepared to jab a needle into a bulging vein on his right forearm.

'You mean the commotion next door?'

He nodded.

'I've given up trying to. I've learnt that some people cannot be reasoned with,' I added, sliding the needle into his vein. 'I imagine I haven't heard the last yelling and screaming tonight.'

'They come out of the woodwork on nights like these. The full moon can drive a man mad. Stay inside and lock the door,' Mr Jones advised.

That sounded like a great idea to me, but

unfortunately hospitals tend to have an open door policy, and anyway, it had already begun . . .

'Someone get security, hurry,' came Amber's voice from beyond the wall.

'Be right back,' I told Mr Jones and rushed out. I needn't have been worried; well, at least not about Amber's safely.

'Put it back on, please, Miss Turner,' Amber pleaded as she tried to wrap a sheet around her patient.

Miss Turner was standing beside her bed completely naked. Her pink dressing gown was lying on the floor next to a far too small hospital nightgown.

'I'm not wearing a fucking sheet. If you can't find anything to fit me, I'll wear fucking nothing.'

The wisest thing to have done at that moment would have been to look away, but my eyes kept being drawn to the multiple loose folds of hanging flesh. It was like a scene from 'Ripley's Believe It or Not', when you know they are about to show you something gruesome, but your morbid curiosity gets the better of you.

'Fucking pervert,' Miss Turner yelled, and made her way towards me.

I was about to be assaulted by a gigantic, intoxicated, naked woman. I briefly thought back to my nursing college days, and tried to remember what they taught you to do in a situation like this. I began to back out of the room, while looking around for some help.

'Hurry up and get security, Amber,' I called out.

'I'm here already,' said a voice behind me.

I glanced over my shoulder to see Jamie.

'I'm not fucking scared of you,' yelled Miss Turner at us. We did not doubt her. She continued to advance, while we men continued to retreat.

'You need to put some clothes on, Miss Turner,' said Jamie.

Good old Jamie, keeping it practical as always.

'Miss Turner, if you don't put your clothes back on we'll have to call the police,' I explained, but this seemed to enrage her more than anything else.

'Fuck the pigs. I'm fucking sick and you're fucking with me. And now you're gonna call the pigs.'

I never got a chance to call the police because she chose this moment to make a run at Jamie and me. We split up, giving each of us a 50 per cent chance of survival, but thankfully she charged straight past us and out into the main corridor of the hospital.

'I've never seen so much flesh move so fast in my life,' said Jamie.

'I never realised it could bounce around so much,' I replied. 'She's all yours, Jamie. Good luck.'

'You've got to be bloody joking. How the hell am I going to stop that? She only has to sit on me and that would be my end.'

He had a point. He really didn't stand a chance.

'At least follow her. Try to stop her from entering any of the wards and I'll call the police.'

Again, I never got a chance to call the police. At that moment an ambulance crew turned up with a teenage girl clutching her stomach and hysterical with pain.

'What's the problem?' I asked.

She didn't say a word, but just screamed louder, all the time rocking back and forth clutching her stomach.

'She said she is having a miscarriage,' Tim, the head paramedic, answered for her. 'But she won't let any of us examine her. We don't have any obs. We haven't checked for any bleeding. Anytime we try to do something, she screams a little louder. She said she only wants a woman to see her.'

'Amber, can I leave her with you?'

Amber may have been new to the emergency room, but she was still an experienced nurse and I knew she could handle one hysterical 16-year-old girl.

'No problem.' She sounded almost relieved to have a somewhat normal patient, with a normal problem, or at least so we thought. I returned to my original patient, Mr Jones. I had a funny suspicion he was relishing the live entertainment.

'Cripes, mate; it's not every day you see something like that. Heck, I've never seen *anything* like it. It's the younger generation, no respect for anything. Such a big lass as well. I wouldn't want to cross her.'

I smothered a smile at his comment — it certainly wasn't the first time I'd heard the older generation lamenting the faults of the young — as Miss Blake, the miscarriage patient, was wheeled past us by Amber.

Trish was standing by and helped Amber place Miss Blake in the bed opposite Mr Jones.

'Poor little thing, what's wrong with her? You better go see to her,' Mr Jones advised me.

Miss Lisa Blake was a tiny looking little thing. She looked at least two or three years younger than 16.

'She's in good hands, Mr Jones. Trish and Amber will sort her out.'

As I examined Mr Jones, I could hear everything that Trish and the young girl had to say.

'I'm bleeding; I'm losing the baby,' sobbed Lisa. 'Oh the pain, please help me. Please help my baby.'

Trish remained calm. In fact, glancing up I'd have said she looked almost bored.

'Before we can help you, we will need a urine sample. I'll show you where the bathroom is.'

'You want me to pee! I'm in pain. Oh . . . ' Lisa clutched her arms around her midsection and began rocking back and forth.

But Trish was not going to budge, and five minutes later, Lisa limped back into the room and handed her urine sample to Trish before crawling back on to the bed.

Trish wasted no time testing the urine.

'I've got some good news for you, Lisa,' said Trish. 'You're not going to lose your baby. Your test was negative: you're not pregnant. And you don't have to worry about bleeding either. There was only a small trace of blood in your urine. You're going to be fine.'

Lisa seemed to have completely forgotten about her pain; she had stopped clutching her stomach and ceased her rocking.

'It's not true. I am pregnant. The test is wrong. I'm in pain.'

Trish stood, unmoved.

Lisa stood up and walked out of the department, without a word or even a glance behind her.

'I told you Trish knows what she's doing,' I said to Mr Jones.

With Mr Jones pain free, his blood samples taken, and observations all up to date, it was time to turn my attention elsewhere. Because there were fewer nurses on during the night shift, you ended up working in all areas of the emergency room. Our department had four areas: minor injuries; moderate illness and injuries; four resuscitation beds for the most serious patients; and triage. With no other patients in resus, I went in search of Amber to see how she was coping. I found her at the front desk.

'Thank goodness you're here. It's turned into a madhouse,' Amber said, gesturing to the full waiting room. With all our time being taken up with Lisa and Miss Turner, the room had been rapidly filling up; people were even sitting on the floor.

'How much longer do we have to wait?' asked a middle-aged woman, who went on to introduce herself as Mrs Kelley. 'We've been here hours.

This is ridiculous. I demand that something be done.'

Mrs Kelley was with her 18-year-old son. He had been out on the town and become involved in what was probably his first punch-up. From the look of him he had a broken nose.

'Probably quite a while longer yet,' I replied. 'You should take your son home and get some rest. There is nothing we can do for him tonight,' I added.

I wasn't in the mood for diplomacy, and this was completely true. There is nothing you can do immediately for a broken nose, even if it is out of shape; you have to wait for the swelling to go down.

Most people in the waiting room seemed to be enjoying the distraction. But I could see Mrs Kelley's hackles rising.

'I demand to be seen immediately or I will be writing to the papers.'

I don't respond well to the word demand and nor do most nurses I know, but I made one more attempt at being polite before turning to address the patient list. 'We have some other patients who need to be seen first.' I turned and walked away, leaving Mrs Kelley to ponder about her potential moment in the media.

Then I heard something surprising. Something I'd never heard before in a hospital, and to this day haven't heard since; I heard singing.

'Why are we waiting? Why are we waiting?'

It started with Mrs Kelley, but soon other

voices joined in. Amber and Trish joined me in the corridor, stunned at what was going on before us.

'Has this ever happened before?' I asked Trish.

'This is a first for me. I feel like I'm in a Monty Python film,' she replied.

'What do we do?' Amber asked.

'Leave them,' Trish said. 'They will soon get sick and tired — '

'Help!' yelled Jamie from afar. 'She's bloody mad. I can't stop her.'

It was coming from behind the waiting room. We rushed out past the singing crowd and into the main hospital corridor to find Jamie being chased by Miss Turner. She was like a rampaging bull, huge, unstoppable and terrifying when provoked.

Jamie reached us, and we tried to form a human barrier.

'Oh shit, she's not stopping,' Jamie and I blurted out in unison.

At least the singing had stopped. The crowd of onlookers in the waiting room had gathered around behind us to see the spectacle. I don't know if they actually thought we could stop this giant pink-slippered woman before she reached them, but there was no way I was going to risk life and limb.

We sidestepped just in time.

Miss Turner collided with the crowd, taking out at least half a dozen onlookers before losing her balance.

If I hadn't seen it with my own eyes, I would never have believed what had just happened. All we could do was laugh. I've never seen a waiting room emptied so quickly. Even Mrs Kelley and her son didn't wait to be seen.

Miss Turner never got to see a doctor; she soon decided to put her clothes back on, and disappeared into the night.

That was four hours of my shift over with, only four more to go.

Russell

'So how do you like our little hospital?' I asked Russell on a rare, quiet afternoon in the emergency room.

'Ach, she's grand, mate. Plenty of action, if ya know what I mean.'

Dr Russell McDonald was our local Scottish import. He had come to New Zealand with one stated purpose.

'I'm gonna fook me way around the world,' Russell had been known to confess to the lads when he'd had a bit too much to drink. 'The lasses here are different to home. At home, if a lass likes ya she'll shag ya, but over here, even if they don't like ya, they'll shag ya anyway. It's great.'

Needless to say, Russell was great for company whenever social occasions arose. And it was probably because he was such a laugh that whenever he fooked up at work, he rarely got in as much trouble as he should have.

Russell had mainly worked in medical wards, where things tend to be slower and more predictable; the things Russell was used to dealing with were the typical problems that make up the bulk of hospital medical admissions, such as the elderly and the difficulties that go along with ageing, from failing lungs, failing hearts, to strokes. It's not exactly exciting like the emergency room, but general medicine like this makes up the backbone of any junior doctor's experience.

Russell also had some experience working in the other areas. All doctors, in both New Zealand and the UK, have to spend some time in each of the main areas of specialisation. The common areas are surgery, paediatrics, obstetrics & gynaecology and orthopaedics. Of course, each of these general fields has many subcategories.

Russell had been working in our hospital for just over a year, six months in general surgery, six months in general medicine, and now the emergency department.

As entertaining as his remarks about wanting to sleep his way around the world were, I wanted a serious answer.

'I'm glad you like the women here, Russ, but how do you like our department so far? How do you find the emergency room?'

'Ach, it's a bit worrying at times, but hey, I've always got you around to keep me out of trouble, eh?' Russell said jokingly as he gave me a wink.

As Russell and I sat around sharing stories, Mrs Reid was brought through to the minor injuries area, clutching her left hand to her chest.

'Can ya check that out for me, mate?' Russell asked me. 'It doesn't look too serious.'

In the two weeks Russell had been in our department, I had discovered that he was the master of delegation, but no one seemed to mind, not even the person getting the instruction.

I sat Mrs Reid down on a bed, and began to

undo the towel she had wrapped around her hand.

'What happened?' I asked.

'The bloody kitchen knife,' she replied, holding out her hand. She had a pretty nasty laceration running the length of her finger.

'We bought one of those new ever-sharp kitchen knives; the ones that sharpen every time you put them away in their sleeves,' Mrs Reid began to explain. 'The damn thing has cut us all. My husband, my son and my daughter.'

I nodded my head in understanding. Generally we try not to suture up fingers. They can heal very well without stitches, often we can get by with paper strips to hold the wound together, but in Mrs Reid's case it was too big a cut.

'It looks like you're going to need a few stitches; I'll get the doctor to take a look.'

Russell didn't mind dealing with anything to do with fingers and toes; they were usually easy to treat.

'Won't take long, Mrs Reid,' Russell began to explain, once he'd taken a look at her injury. 'A few stitches and you'll be on your way home. I'll pop in a bit of local anaesthetic and you won't feel a thing.'

With this, Russell began to get things ready.

I watched as Russell grabbed the wrong vial from a cupboard, and briefly debated whether I should say something. Just because I know how to fix a particular injury one way, doesn't mean it's the only way. I wanted to give him the benefit of the doubt because maybe he knew something I didn't, and I also didn't want to make him look incompetent in front of a patient.

However, I eventually had to step in.

'Um, Russ, here's some different anaesthetic,' I said, opening a second cupboard, 'without adrenaline. Which one do you want?'

If you use adrenaline-laced anaesthetic on a finger, it can cut off the blood supply. Russell took a second look at the vial he was holding, before quickly exchanging it for the right kind.

'I think I'll take the one without adrenaline this time, no need to go overboard,' he said with a smile and a wink as if he had things completely under control, even though Mrs Reid could have lost her finger if he'd gone ahead.

'Just a little sting, then you won't feel a thing,' Russell said to Mrs Reid. 'It will go numb pretty quick.'

Russell held Mrs Reid's hand in his, with her palm facing down, and began to inject the anaesthetic into the base of her finger.

'Nearly done, Mrs Reid,' Russ said. 'Can you just turn your hand over and I'll numb the other side of the finger?'

Like the good and trusting patient she was, Mrs Reid did as she was instructed. Russell began to inject the other side of the finger.

Something didn't look right. Again, I wanted to say something, but hesitated because I didn't want him to look foolish. Surely Russell couldn't be that stupid. I felt it must have been a technique I didn't know. I knew he'd be pissed if I interrupted again.

'Interesting technique, Russ,' I said, trying to prod him into explaining himself.

'Ach, it's nothing, pretty basic really,' he explained. 'It's the sort of thing anyone could do. You can't go wrong, laddie.'

He touched the tip of the third finger from the thumb.

'You shouldn't be feeling a thing, Mrs Reid,' he said as if he had casually performed a small miracle.

'Well, I don't feel a thing, but what about my middle finger? It's still pretty sore.'

The triumphant look faded from Russell's face. He looked at me accusingly.

'How could you let me do the wrong finger? You watched me do it and said nothing.'

There wasn't a lot I could say. I should have spoken up, but it was his bloody fault, not mine.

'I'm terribly sorry, Mrs Reid,' Russell said. 'I feel a bit of a fool. Give me a moment and I'll fix it up.' Luckily for Russell, Mrs Reid wasn't upset, in fact she laughed. It was the Russell charm at work. No one could resist it.

Two days later, Russell still hadn't completely forgiven me.

'Ya stood and watched me fook things up. Fookin' lot of good you were.'

He said it jokingly, but the Dr Russell McDonald charm was wearing a tad thin on me.

'Get over it, Russ. You screwed up, not me.'

Later that afternoon, Miss Hope was brought in by ambulance.

'She fell off her horse. She's a race horse trainer. The horse stood on her thigh. It looks pretty bad,' the paramedic explained to Russell as we all helped transfer her from the stretcher on to the emergency room trolley, 'but I don't think she's ruptured an artery.'

Miss Hope chose that moment to scream out in pain.

'Arrrgh, hell, oh bloody hell.' She then began to weep.

'We've given her ten milligrams of morphine, but when we move her she screams in agony,' explained the paramedic.

There were muffled gasps of horror when the extent of Miss Hope's injury was revealed. Her right thigh was most definitely U-shaped. I glanced briefly at Russell to gauge how he was coping. I'll give him credit, he looked calm and in control.

'What next?' I asked Russell.

I knew what to do, as did the nurses around me, so we got to work monitoring her pulse and blood pressure. Someone put in another IV line and took blood for a cross-match, another got a bag of fluids ready.

'Let's leave her leg briefly. I need to check her out,' Russell said as he began at Miss Hope's head and worked his way down, checking for any other injury.

Thank goodness he said the right thing, because after his last screw-up, I needed to be reassured that he knew what he was doing.

Whenever a serious admission comes into hospital with an obvious injury, it's easy to focus on that one injury because it's so glaringly obvious. But what mustn't be forgotten is a check of the rest of the body, to make sure there are no other injuries. For all we knew, Miss

Hope could have been briefly knocked unconscious when she fell. It would be pretty awful if we fixed her leg up, and missed a small but lethal bleed in the brain.

Once Russell was satisfied that Miss Hope had no other injury, he began to deal with her pain.

'What do you think, Dr McDonald?' I asked, not really sure what would be best for Miss Hope as the intravenous morphine wasn't as effective as I had hoped.

'Femoral block, that'll do the trick, then off to theatre.'

A femoral block is an injection of pain killer into the groin on the affected side. The anaesthetic is extremely effective as it completely blocks the pain. It's short lasting, only an hour or two, but it would be enough to keep Miss Hope comfortable until she was taken to theatre.

Russell really seemed to be doing a good job. The calm and correct way he was dealing with things was putting not just me at ease, but the patient as well.

'I'll leave you to it,' I said to Russell, having got the equipment he needed to perform the procedure. 'But I'll be at the bed opposite if you need me. Just sing out and I'll be right there.'

Ten minutes passed and Russell hadn't reached out for help. All must have gone well. I poked my head through the curtain.

'You shouldn't be feeling a thing,' Russell was saying to Miss Hope while gently touching her left foot.

I couldn't believe what I was hearing.

'I can't feel a thing,' she replied, 'but my right

291

leg is still bloody agony.'

Russell looked up at me, an expression of horror on his face.

'When will it help my right leg? It had better be bloody well soon. It's unbearable.'

How would Russell charm his way out of this one?

'I think you need a bit more,' Russell began, 'just another small injection, and then you'll be fine.'

I couldn't speak up in front of the patient. The damage had been done but at least with another injection the patient would still get some relief. But in the interests of future patient safety and my own liability, I had to do something.

Once Miss Hope was wheeled off to theatre, Russell approached me, a big, albeit forced, smile on his face. But there was no Russell wink, and he wouldn't look me in the eye.

'Fookin' great,' he said. 'Have ya told the boss yet?'

I didn't like to be the one to turn my friend in, but this was serious.

'Sorry, Russ, but you really messed up. At least he doesn't know about the finger episode. It's your first screw-up as far as he is concerned,' I said, trying to look on the bright side.

'Well, thanks anyway.'

Russell was taking this better than I expected.

'I can't believe I got the wrong leg. What is wrong with me?'

I didn't say anything; we both knew that this could be the end of his time in the emergency room.

The senior doctor of the emergency room reacted reasonably well, with only a little shouting, and some mild threats to end Russell's career.

Nevertheless, the following week, Russell went to work in the medical ward where he would be in familiar territory. The emergency room is not for everyone, and it's not a place where you can bluff your way through. The emergency room is often the home of the most experienced doctors and nurses, who have spent plenty of time in the core areas of medicine. People like this don't accept egos or incompetence. They can't afford to when people's lives are at stake.

All for a plate of sandwiches

'Where're my boots? You've stolen my bloody boots,' Mr Crump shouted as he was wheeled past. 'Did you hear me? Where're my fucking boots?'

Tom the paramedic stood at the head of the trolley. He'd heard it all before and was now impervious to Mr Crump's tirades. In fact, as an experienced paramedic, he'd heard a lot worse. Mr Crump was just being his normal self, a miserable old drunken sod.

'Let me guess, the garden again?' I asked Tom as we transferred Mr Crump from the trolley to the bed.

'How'd you guess? Oh, that's right it's raining. This is the third time in two months, isn't it, Mr Crump?' Tom replied, with a wry smile.

'I didn't bloody well ask to come here. You've no bloody right. Where's my boots, ya thief?'

'Just doing my job.' Tom shrugged his shoulders, and turned to me. 'His neighbours found him unconscious in the garden; said they could hear him partying all night. At around eight o'clock next morning, he headed out to the garden and began digging.'

Mr Crump was freezing to touch; he was lucky to be alive. It may have been late summer, but there was a nip in the air and the rain coming down outside was torrential.

'Mr Crump, your neighbours probably saved

294

your life. If they hadn't kept an eye on you, you'd probably be dead on your lawn.' I paused briefly, wondering why I bothered to explain, but it was my nature to give Mr Crump a chance to redeem himself.

'Bah! What bullshit. I'm not soft like you. I've been doing this for 50 years and I'm as tough as nails. A little rain won't hurt me. Just get me my boots and I'll be outta here,' Mr Crump said in disgust.

'The only reason you're still here, is because every time you've passed out in the garden, in bad weather, your neighbours have called the ambulance. It's not our fault you can't handle your booze.'

Of course, I was well aware the old boy could outdrink any of us. He had all the visible signs of a serious long-term drinker: rheumy eyes that could still see, but no longer cared what they saw; a huge, red, bulbous mass that once was a nose; a wiry body, grotesquely distorted by his protruding beer belly; and worst of all, the overwhelming smell of rotten teeth, mixed with blood from his bleeding gums, combined again with spirits and beer. When people regularly drink too much the alcohol affects every organ in the body. At the levels Mr Crump drank, he was constantly poisoning himself, from his brain to the tiniest blood vessel. Long-term heavy drinkers develop swollen noses due to the damage caused by and dilatory effect of alcohol on the blood vessels. Over time, it's the liver that takes the brunt of alcohol abuse. It keeps on getting bigger, as it has to work overtime to remove the toxins from the body. It's not unusual to see people with a liver twice the size of a normal one, hence the swollen stomach.

Then, of course, there is the effect on the brain. I've seen some middle-aged men showing signs of dementia. It's not reversible.

Mr Crump sat up in bed and looked at me expectantly.

'Well, I'm here now so you might as well make yourself useful.'

His tone had softened a little. I felt the corners of my mouth forming a smile — I knew the routine well.

'One or two sugars?' I asked.

'Two, and don't forget the sandwiches; I'm starving.'

Tom looked at me and rolled his eyes. He too was familiar with the process.

Mr Crump inhaled the sandwiches.

'Any more?' he asked, picking crumbs off the plate.

Four ham and cheese sandwiches, four slices of toast dripping with butter and honey, and a cup of coffee later, Mr Crump sat back on his bed rubbing his belly, a contented look on his face.

'Where's me boots? Be a good lad and get me boots would ya, I'd better be on my way.'

I half-heartedly tried to dissuade Mr Crump from leaving, as he technically needed to see a doctor.

'I don't need to see a flaming doctor. I need to get home, back to me garden. I'm as fit as a fiddle,' he protested.

From past experience, I knew the battle was never going to be won and I made sure that Mr Crump signed the self-discharge form, just in case he dropped dead when he walked out the door.

Sometimes it felt like nearly all my time and energy was spent dealing with the consequences of alcohol misuse. From Thursday through to Sunday night, I would have been willing to bet my monthly salary that every shift would bring in an alcohol-related patient, whether they were drunk themselves, or the victim of someone else's drunkenness. Maybe they were all victims in one way or another, they just didn't know it.

My experiences were sometimes amusing, tragic, horrible, or even scary, but never boring. The people affected by alcohol came from all walks of life, and from all corners of the world.

Whether it is the Mr Crumps of the world, or a first-time drinker, I've found patients come in two main categories: there are your nice drunks and then there are your mean drunks.

In fact it's amazing how much Brits and Kiwis have in common when it comes to alcohol-related presentations to the emergency room. Here's a sample of some of the colourful characters, and the typical types of patients and problems.

VI

The nice drunk

Peter had been celebrating his eighteenth birthday. He might have been fine if he hadn't been peer-pressured into playing one of the most challenging drinking games I'd heard of in quite a while. The victim — sorry, the birthday boy — had to drink half a pint of beer faster than any of the people at his party. If he didn't beat the person in front of him, he had to keep on trying until he won, before moving on to the next guest. There were 15 friends celebrating Peter's birthday.

When Peter did not return from a vomiting spell in the toilet, his friends had gone searching for him, only to find him lying on the bathroom floor, unable to be roused. An ambulance was soon called.

'I'm sorry, sir, Mr Nurse, sir. I'm so sorry to be a burden,' Peter slurred, before completely missing the bowl we'd placed beside his head and throwing up on to the floor.

'I'm really sorry; I'll clean it up,' he offered, rolling off the bed.

Peter's last words were blurred as he gave up and decided to doze off for a bit, resting his head in his own sick.

Tracey, my comrade in arms that Friday night, came over and, with a firm and none too gentle grip, helped haul Peter up off the floor.

'Fuck, I'm really sorry.'

Peter slumped between Tracey and me, his eyes closed, his face ashen.

'Hey Peter, cut out the bad language, there are children in here, mate,' I said.

'Fuck I'm sor . . . shit, sorry, fuck. So sorry.'

The nice drunk tries to cause as little disturbance as possible. Believe it or not Peter really was a nice drunk. He couldn't help being a burden — he was so intoxicated that he was a danger to himself — but at least he meant well.

Not many people as drunk as Peter worry about their language or worry about being a nuisance.

Plus, he gave the other dozen patients in the room a distraction from the fact that they had been waiting for three hours to see the doctor — although it probably wasn't the best scene for the ten-year-old girl sitting with her mother.

Peter's treatment was pretty straightforward: intravenous fluids, a dose of medicine to help with any nausea, a quick review by the doctor, then home. It may seem we were being overly nice — some would say that he deserved a hangover — but to be honest, we just wanted him sobered up so we could get him out of the department as soon as possible.

The hardest part is often the phone call to mum and dad. Even though Peter was an adult, just, at his age it's still usually the parents that come to the rescue.

'Is this Mr Birch?' It was four in the morning, and on my third phone call I got an answer.

'Er, yes . . . Who is this?'

'I'm calling from the emergency department.

I'm one of the nursing staff. Everything is okay, but we have your son here with us.'

Any leftover sleep-induced confusion evaporated from his voice. 'What's happened? Is he okay? What's going on?'

'Peter had a bit too much to drink tonight — ' I never got a chance to finish.

'The bloody idiot, how bad is he? Was he in a fight?'

'He's okay, he hasn't been hurt, but he did pass out. He's awake now, and the doctor said he's well enough to go home. Can you come and collect him?'

Dad said he'd be here in 20 minutes.

'He's going to kill me.' Peter had sobered up enough to appreciate the seriousness of the situation. 'Hell, I'm so sorry. What have I done?'

I felt sympathetic to his cause. We all make mistakes (especially when we're teenagers) and as bad as he felt now, it really wasn't the end of the world.

'Think of this as a lesson. You got lucky. There's been no permanent harm done. It's a good sign you feel bad about your actions. Not everyone does. Oh, and as for your parents, well, they might be angry, but they'll be even more relieved that you're okay.'

Peter was lucky, because his dad seemed really nice. He didn't yell, he was calm, and once he realised his son was fine, he even managed a brief chuckle about the whole situation. I could see that wasn't the reaction Peter had expected. Thankfully, I've seen a lot of teenagers surprised, in a good way, by the unexpected responses of their parents.

Sadly, though, not everyone has parents to pick them up when they get drunk. Some people live their lives around alcohol, and usually end up paying the price.

The regular drunk

'Where's Mr Finnerty?' asked Tracey, looking around anxiously, 'He's supposed to be in cubicle 4 but he's gone missing.'

This was not the first time we'd lost this particular patient. He was notorious for getting lost trying to find the toilet.

Mr Finnerty was a homeless, 60-year-old Irish alcoholic who was brought in every couple of months, because he had drunk himself unconscious and a Good Samaritan had decided to call an ambulance after tripping over him on the street.

'Check the toilets, then the kitchen. He either needs a pee or he's woken up hungry,' I suggested.

The kitchen was empty, as were the toilets.

'He won't have left,' said Tracey, as we reconvened. 'He must be around the ward somewhere.'

Mr Finnerty always slept until morning and left after coffee and toast. For people like Mr Finnerty it must be a bit like Christmas to sleep in a bed and have a hot drink.

Mr Finnerty's treatment differed slightly to less hardened drinkers; he would be given an infusion of vitamins, including vitamin B, which alcoholics generally lack, and some diazepam tablets, which help the body relax and cope with the stress of going without alcohol for a night.

Tracey continued to pace around the emergency room, peering into every nook and cranny, but she needn't have bothered; a nasty trauma was wheeled into the resuscitation bed and Mr Finnerty seemed to materialise out of thin air.

'Need any help? I've got a spare kidney if anyone needs one.'

Of course, Mr Finnerty was only trying to help, but it really wasn't the sort of help that the doctor needed. Tracey firmly, but gently, grasped his arm and marched him back to his cubicle. Mr Finnerty glanced over his shoulder and winked at me, obviously enjoying the attention.

The sight of a gorgeous, petite blonde telling off a 60-year-old, bearded, intoxicated Irishman who was pretending to act remorseful was rather memorable. It was almost cute.

When morning came around, there was no one to call to come and pick up Mr Finnerty. He was discharged home, which happened to be under a nearby bridge.

The unconscious drunk

The unconscious drunk is a valuable sub-category of the nice drunk. They count as nice, because they can't do anything to offend you (although they can be the hardest work as patients; an unprotected airway is such a nuisance). A truly unconscious drunk cannot complain, cannot be violent, and doesn't need assistance walking to the toilet as they've already been doubly incontinent in their bed. Best of all they don't need anaesthetic when suturing up lacerations or manipulating broken bones.

Thankfully, with experience comes the ability to spot an unconscious drunk, as opposed to someone simply asleep. An experienced nurse uses modern medical technology alongside their highly developed skills when assessing an unconscious patient. In the case of the unconscious drunk, we use pain.

Yes, you read right, we administer different levels of pain to see exactly *how* unconscious a patient is. There are different levels of unconsciousness and it's important that we know exactly how serious the situation may be. We need to know exactly how much stimulus is needed to rouse someone.

1. Sound: do they respond to noise? They may open their eyes briefly when you call their name, or make a slurred sound.

2. Movement: maybe a gentle shake of the shoulder is enough to get a response, as is often the case when someone is simply asleep.

3. Fingernails: there are a number of ways a patient can respond to us squeezing their fingernails against a solid object. They might open their eyes and shout. They might pull away their hand, moan, but keep their eyes shut, or open them just briefly then fall immediately back to sleep. In the worst cases, they don't flinch, don't even flicker their eyes, don't make a noise. Alternatively, they might wake up and try to punch you.

4. Sternum: after the fingernails, comes rubbing of the knuckles across the patient's sternum. This works rather well, and I've woken up a number of deeply-under patients this way.

5. Eyes: the final option is to press a point on the inside of the eye socket. I haven't had to use this option often, but I know it to be effective.

If none of these methods get you the desired response from the patient, then the situation becomes much more serious. Usually an anaesthetist is called to decide exactly what to do.

It is not uncommon for these patients to be intubated. This means a tube is stuck down the throat, and the patient is placed on a ventilator.

Most of us will know how to look after our

friends when they've had too much to drink; to roll them on their side to protect their airway. In the case of the truly unconscious, the risk is the same, but there is no knowing when they may rouse, or even what they've consumed, so drastic measures are taken to protect the airway.

The lucky drunk

'Now don't be hard on yourself, but I told you so. You wasted your time, and mine.'

Mr Riley was sitting on the edge of his bed, waving his finger in the face of the paramedic who had brought him in.

'And to think you could be helping someone really in need, and instead you're here with me. I'm flattered, really, but you shouldn't have.'

'You fell from the first floor of your house on to your front lawn. You're lucky you didn't break something. Hell, you're lucky you're still alive,' I said as I continued cleaning up the mixture of dried and fresh blood from Mr Riley's forehead. I'd been busy cleaning him for the last ten minutes. The paramedic had stayed with us as he had wanted to see how badly Mr Riley was injured, especially since he'd refused a neck brace and insisted on being wheeled in on a chair instead of a bed.

Aside from 12 fresh sutures in his head, Mr Riley had no other signs of injury. His friends insisted he wasn't knocked out, and the only reason they called the ambulance was because he was bleeding all over the carpet. In the end, Mr Riley went home, against medical advice, and back to enjoy the party.

Mr Riley was fortunate, because being drunk enabled him to survive an accident that would otherwise kill, or at least seriously injure, most sober people.

Take Mrs Reese, who was occupying the bed next to Mr Riley. Mrs Reese was an elderly lady who had fallen off her chair. She broke her hip.

Part of the reason for this seeming injustice is to do with being relaxed. When you're sober and fall, you are aware of what is going on, and you tense. Ironically, tensing is what increases the likelihood of damage.

Of course, I very much doubt Mr Riley would have fallen from his balcony if he had not been drinking.

The mean drunk

And now we come to the other main category of drunk, the mean drunk, also known as the pain in the arse drunk. These are particularly easy to spot.

'Come on, Rick; open your eyes,' I said to Rick. But apparently Rick wasn't interested in waking up as he continued to lie on the bed unmoving.

'He was asleep when we found him; he was rousable to voice,' said the paramedic who had brought him in. 'He's only been like this since we wheeled him through the hospital doors. I suspect he's acting.'

I watched as the doctor assessed the patient. Dr Wilson began to do the usual tests to assess level of consciousness. Pinching, poking, rubbing, all to no effect.

'Well, either he's a good actor, or he's really unconscious,' he said.

'Let me have a go, just to be sure,' I volunteered. I prided myself on being able to wake up most cases that presented in the emergency room.

Dr Wilson stood aside as I went about the job of administering medicinal pain.

I had no success either.

'We'd better get him undressed and put on a monitor quickly then,' said Dr Wilson.

'It looks like he might be unconscious after

all,' I added, but I wasn't entirely convinced.

I took some scissors and went in to cautiously cut off his shirt.

At the first snip, Rick sat up suddenly and swung a fist in my general direction.

'You've cut my fucking shirt. What the fuck you do that for?'

I had been ready for it and dodged easily out of the way.

'That cost 50 fucking quid. You gonna pay for that?'

I shrugged my shoulders. 'You're supposed to be unconscious. Just following hospital protocol,' I replied.

Rick leapt up off the bed, ripping out his IV line in the process. With blood dripping down his arm, he lunged towards me, but Dr Wilson and the paramedic were ready and wrestled him back on to the bed.

Rick could see he was outnumbered and stayed down, but not without sharing his knowledge of the English language.

'Now, we'll let you go as long as you promise not to try to hit any of us,' Dr Wilson explained. 'If you try anything else, you'll be spending time with some friendly police officers.'

Bare chest heaving from anger, Rick wrapped his £50 shirt around his bleeding arm and stormed out of the department.

Rick was a fine example of a mean drunk: obnoxious, loud, violent, and a complete pain in the arse. Rick was not the first person to feign unconsciousness and was only one of God knows how many to become violent.

Of course, in some ways, an aggressive drunk patient makes our job much easier — anyone able to stand up and make violent threats is well enough to be forcibly removed from the department.

The changed drunk

'This is bullshit,' James exclaimed while glancing around the relatively empty waiting room. 'I'm a lawyer and I know my rights. You can't keep me waiting. You're fucking with me, that's what you're doing.'

James took a step towards me, his fists clenching and unclenching. Thankfully, his friend, Steven, grabbed him around the shoulders. 'Hey, James, calm down, mate; they're only trying to help.'

'I've never seen him like this. I'm really sorry. He's not the aggressive type,' Steven said, turning from me, and firmly pushing James back down on to his seat. 'I've known him all my life; he's not a trouble maker.'

There is one exception to the dichotomy of nasty and nice drunks — one which all nurses must watch out for: the mean drunk who has experienced a knock to the head.

With James's hair covered in blood, and his left eye nearly swollen shut, Steven's words sparked off alarm bells. 'Follow me.'

'Thank fuck for that,' said James, as I laid him down on a bed.

'Tell me what happened?' I asked.

James looked up at me, not bothering to brush aside the blood-matted hair that covered his good eye.

'What the fuck do you think happened? I got

assaulted, that's what the fuck happened.'

Steven held up his hand, motioning for James to be silent.

'We were having a night out on the town, you know; had a bit too much to drink and all — ' Steven began.

I interrupted.

'How much is 'too much'? I need a rough estimate,' I said.

'Well, we finished off a bottle of vodka; maybe half a dozen beers each,' he said.

'That's a lot of booze for two people,' I offered.

Steven responded with a mirthless laugh. 'That was before we went to the pub.'

James made a moaning sound and promptly vomited a litre or two of alcohol over himself. I offered Steven a pair of latex gloves.

'I need you to help. Let's get him undressed while you finish your story. I just want to know how he got hurt.'

Steven looked at the gloves like they were diseased, but slowly put them on.

'Well, some guy kicked up a fight. James got hit a few times in the head. The security guys broke it up and threw the guy who started it out. We left the pub about half an hour later and he was waiting for us and hit James over the head with a brick. Security caught him and called the police.'

'Did James lose consciousness?' I asked.

'No. I mean, he fell to the ground, but he was awake, on his hands and knees. Took a few minutes to stand up, but he got up. Cops said we should get him checked out. So here we are.'

As we began to undress James he pushed away my hands.

'Let me sleep,' he mumbled, his eyes closed.

Steven looked, his eyebrows raised, seeking direction.

'Keep going, we need to get him in a gown,' I instructed.

James didn't try to resist this time and two minutes later he was in a white hospital robe. I gently wrapped a bandage around his head to stop the sluggish thread of blood still trickling down his face.

'James, can you hear me?' I asked. No response.

I rubbed my knuckles over his chest. His eyes opened briefly and his arms came up and tried to push me away.

'Fuck off,' he mumbled, then instantly went back to sleep.

'He can normally handle his booze. I'm so sorry,' Steven began to apologise.

'Don't apologise; I think it's the knock to the head. I need to get the doctor now. Don't go anywhere,' I instructed. 'The doctor will want to ask you some questions, probably the same ones I've already asked you.'

The only response Dr Wilson could get from James was an automatic, brief but wild lashing out of his arms to deep pain stimuli.

'How long has he been like this?' Dr Wilson demanded.

'He was awake five minutes ago; he only arrived about 15 minutes ago. He's deteriorated within that time.'

Defensively, my voice rose an octave or two. Dr Wilson gave me a brief smile.

'Good job,' he said as we began wheeling James through to the resuscitation area.

The problem with alcohol is that it can very easily disguise the signs of more serious damage. The two most dangerous symptoms of a head injury happen to be two of the more common consequences of alcohol consumption: altered levels of consciousness and aggressive, abusive behaviour.

With James, I could so easily have got it wrong and it sometimes knots my stomach. I could have made the abusive, obnoxious drunk sit and wait in the waiting room; it was certainly tempting. He would have fallen asleep, or at least that is what it would have seemed like. He might have been dead by the time someone went to wake him up. Perhaps having vomited and choked to death, or from the bruise in his head continuing to bleed.

Because of the potential to get it wrong with a simple head injury where alcohol is involved, staff will often put up with some pretty bad behaviour.

In James's case he was intubated, and taken for a CT scan of his head, which showed a bruise inside the skull. Only after 24 hours in the intensive care unit was he awake, taken off a ventilator and transferred to a regular ward. He made a full recovery.

The final draught

So there you are. If you ever find yourself on a Friday night in your local emergency room, and you've had a bit to drink, there are two things I want you to remember: be nice, and be honest.

You see, being a nice drunk isn't about making my life easier (although that's nice too), it's about making your recovery that much quicker. If you listen to our advice, don't fight against us, and let us do our job, you'll get the care you need.

Be honest about how much you've had and how you got hurt. We're not here to judge. It's about helping us to make the right diagnosis, and helping us to give you the treatment you need.

Epilogue:

Reflections on a life of nursing

The dos and don'ts
of being a patient

It's been a long time since I began my career as a naïve, young, outnumbered male nurse. Some days I wonder how I've lasted so long, other times I ask myself why I chose to stay so long. The answer is simple, it's because of you.

Now don't get soppy on me, what I'm trying to say is that you keep my job interesting. You can make me laugh, cry, tear my hair out in frustration, shudder in disgust, beam with pride, or even make me lose my cool. This job is never boring, and it is rarely easy. Sometimes, every day can be a challenge. But there are some things patients can do to make my job easier. And, by making my life easier, you will ultimately make your hospital stay easier.

So, if ever you find yourself in the emergency room, or even admitted to a ward, here are some simple things to remember:

1. Listen to our advice. If we say 'Don't have a shower because you've just had your appendix out', then don't have a shower. I've lost count of the times I've waited outside the cubicle and caught a collapsed young adult.

2. Be sober. It's rarely just a matter of being intoxicated, there's nearly always some other complicating factor, like being found unconscious, so we can't find out the history. This may mean spending the night in the emergency room, which neither of us wants.

3. Have a sense of humour. Sometimes there is no point in getting angry. Laughter really can be the best medicine.

4. Be nice and be patient. I don't really have time to serve you tea and biscuits. However, I have done it before, and I will probably do it again. But if you're not nice, I won't do those extra things that aren't really part of my job, but can make your stay much more pleasant.

5. No matter what hospital you find yourself in, never start a conversation with 'I demand . . . ' The triage nurse has all the power, and it is she (or he) who decides who will see the doctor next. If your problem really isn't urgent, you're liable to find yourself waiting a very long time.

6. Don't withhold medicine. It's surprising how many patients come to hospital for some minor ache or pain, without having taken any pain killers. The common assumption is that the doctor will want to see just how bad things are. But you're likely to find the doctor prescribes simple paracetamol.

7. Be honest. We're not policemen. If you've taken drugs, we won't report you. We won't even tell your parents. Being honest may also save your life.

8. Remember Murphy's Law. Don't be difficult, picky, demanding or ungrateful. The bad luck experienced by unpleasant patients and families is uncanny. If equipment is going to malfunction, or an unexplainable complication is going to occur, or we are going to run out of a particular medication, it almost always happens to the patients already making a fuss.

The big difference

I've learnt a lot about being a nurse over the past 16 years, but what have I learnt about being a *male* nurse? Actually, that Cherie, my first mentor, was right: nurses are nurses first, and women or men second.

But it can't be denied, there are some differences that are too big to avoid. Most importantly, there is a big difference between a male and a female nurse when it comes to private parts. Hold on a moment, you're probably thinking something rather basic, but what I'm referring to isn't quite so simple. It's when dealing with the private parts of *patients* that things become a bit complicated.

I've known of male patients asking female nurses to help them put their penises in a urine bottle. The experienced nurse happily grabs a sharp-toothed pair of forceps to seize the helpless man's member and insert it into the bottle. Unsurprisingly, there is never a repeat show. This, however, has never happened to me.

Some would say that makes me lucky, but then again, I've got some unique problems that not all of my female colleagues, or even some of my fellow male nurses, appreciate. In fact, I've even been told that I'm unprofessional, even that I should not be a nurse, because there are some things I won't do.

Actually, there's only one thing I *won't* do,

and that is female catheterisation.

Yes, females do this procedure on men, so why shouldn't I do it on women? In most places I've worked in, I've helped the women out by doing their men, while they do my women. It works for me, and the staff, but most importantly it works for the patient.

I've been called a hypocrite and a sexist for having this attitude, but then I sometimes wonder who the biggest hypocrite is. If gender does not matter to a nursing professional, then why am I always allowed to shower little old ladies (a safe age seeming to be 60 plus) but never allowed to shower a 20-something woman.

Just for the record, I'm not trying to suggest I *should* be allowed to bathe attractive young patients, but if I'm sexist for feeling a bit old fashioned about some things, then those nurses who think I should do it all, and that gender does not matter, could be called ageist.

To further my defence, to perform certain procedures on a woman, requires a female chaperone anyway, so that chaperone might as well go ahead and do the procedure herself, and I can do her a favour another time.

With most procedures, though, it's just a case of accounting for the fact that I'm a guy, and considering what I can do to make myself and my patients as comfortable as possible, whether that be a strategically placed towel, or simply knocking on a door before walking into a patient's room.

If this is to be considered a weakness on my part, so be it, but I had to learn very early how to deal with sensitive issues. I was, after all, a new graduate accidentally placed in a gynaecology ward.

However you look at it, gender does matter, but not always in a negative way.

Often just by being what we are, a woman or a man, we can bring out the different sides of a patient. The company of your own gender is not to be underestimated. Older male patients often love to be treated as 'one of the boys', it helps them to open up, and I've heard some pretty amusing stories bringing laughter into difficult situations that I don't believe they'd have relayed to a female nurse. After all, isn't this what the job is about — making a patient's stay a bit more comfortable, a bit more bearable and a bit more humane?

So yes, there is a difference between the private parts of the male and female nursing staff, but I do believe we can make them work together . . . to, er, bring out the best in everyone, of course.

How we do it

Nurses aren't made of stone, although patients might think so. The secret is to learn to mouth breathe. Not sure what on earth I'm on about? Let me be explicit.

From bowel motions and contaminated wounds, to flesh eating infections, I've smelt a lot of horrible things during my career. I used to gag, but you have to rise above it, for your sake and the patient's. Mouth breathing really does help, but then sometimes the thought of breathing in freely what your nose would naturally filter is enough to make you retch itself. In these cases, all you can do is try holding your breath. But, more likely, you have to grin and bear it.

Sometimes when a nurse knows what to expect, there's an opportunity to bring in air freshener. The stuff hospitals use actually eats the odour (or so I've been told). The only problem with this is trying to be discreet; it doesn't look good if you enter the room spraying every square inch of space from doorway to a patient's backside. (I admit I may have been guilty of this, but only in the most extreme of cases.)

It's not always a smell but a sight which is offensive. It's pretty common for elderly men to put their dentures in a glass of water for the night. What is not so ordinary a sight is for them to drink the glass of water once they've put their teeth back in for breakfast. You'd think the prospect of so many floating things in the glass really would be a turn-off.

More often than anything, it's the thought of the substances themselves that's the worst. One of my most distressful moments as a nurse came about when emptying a particularly unpleasant bedpan into the sluice. A drop bounced up and landed on my lower lip. While pulling my lower lip down to my navel, I rinsed it with every caustic substance I could find — I think I probably caused more harm to myself from the acerbic cleaners than if I'd actually swallowed the damn thing. Fortunately my vaccinations were all up to date, and that ward has since put in splash guards.

On another occasion, one of my patients, a poor confused old lady, was having a terrible time with her piles. Her problem was exacerbated by a bad case of diarrhoea. The discomfort caused her to wander around the ward. She usually left a trail wherever she went. It wasn't pleasant having to constantly chase after her and clean up the mess, but sometimes you just have to get on with the job. Fortunately, I solved the problem (temporarily at least) by using some lignocaine gel. This is an anaesthetic gel we usually use when catheterising patients. It worked wonders for her. The poor soul couldn't stop thanking me. I was just relieved she felt better, and I could get on with more savoury tasks.

Unsurprisingly, many patients are embarrassed by these side effects of their illnesses. The variety of wounds a patient can present with is endless, as are the types of bowel movements that can be passed. What many people don't realise is that an experienced nurse can actually sometimes make a diagnosis just from seeing, or smelling, a patient's excreta. Things like gastric bleeds, sweet smelling wound infections and cloudy urine can be the key to an important treatment.

As I said before, I'm not made of stone, but like most nurses I know, after some practice, I've developed the willpower to overcome almost anything.

The best of the NHS

I'm not unique, but I have done what many of my colleagues never have, which is to not only work in different countries, but also in dozens of different hospitals, in a vast variety of fields. I'm a classic example of the saying Jack of all trades, master of none.

I believe that what I've experienced has changed me for the better. I try not to make rash judgements, because I've seen many different ways of looking at and doing things. I've been through all of the bad and ugly stuff that your average nurse goes through during the course of their career. Yet for every negative experience, there have been so many more positive ones, and for every sad occasion, there were just as many happy and inspiring moments. I hope I've managed to balance this out, and given you an insight into my world. I would love to think that maybe something positive can come from sharing my highs and lows.

Over the course of my 16 years as a practising nurse, I've come to realise that often the truly meaningful and life changing moments of this job happen when we, as nurses, have the time to do what we know we are capable of. On those occasions when we have enough staff, who are not burdened by excessive workloads, we have the opportunity to truly look after the whole person. When this happens, its all good.

Day 1

'Who's going to look after me dog? I'm not sick. I don't need to be here.'

Mr Blake was partially right. Medically, he was pretty healthy for an 80-year-old man. But the thing about public healthcare and the people that work within the system is that we don't just look at the physical symptoms and diagnosis. We look at the complete picture, and try to do what we can for the whole person.

'Is there anyone we can call to check on your house? Feed your dog?' I asked.

'Me and Rascal only got each other. He'll be worried if I'm not home.'

Aside from Rascal, Mr Blake had been living alone for the last 15 years since his wife died, and like many aged men living on their own, he was stubborn when it came to accepting any help, or even to admitting that he needed any.

'Are there any family members we can contact; maybe they can come and help.'

'Now don't go calling any of my kids. They're busy enough with their own families.'

'I'm sure they'd want to know you're in hospital.'

Mr Blake scowled, his pleasant demeanour rapidly evaporating.

'What about your neighbour, the one that called the ambulance? Perhaps I can give him a call. I'm sure he'll be more than happy to feed your dog.'

'How many times do I have to tell you? I'm not staying. Rascal needs me.'

Mr Blake had fallen over on the ice outside his house and received a few grazes to his hands and face. The neighbour had witnessed the fall and made a call to the paramedics. When the paramedics had arrived, they'd had a chance to see inside Mr Blake's home, and it had been a worrying sight.

Everything they'd seen inside the house pointed towards a man not coping on his own: piles of unwashed dishes in the kitchen; no food in the cupboards except for some stale bread and baked beans. The clothes in his room, as well as those he wore and had packed in his suitcase, were in desperate need of a clean. Worst of all, the house was like a fridge. Mr Blake had a small plug-in heater by an armchair piled with blankets. They thought this was probably where he slept each night.

Then of course there was the dog. He was nice enough (at least the paramedics had said he was) but the place reeked of faeces, the furniture covered in animal hair, and like his master, the poor creature looked underfed and filthy.

Mr Blake needed to stay with us for his own good, but technically we could not stop him discharging himself if he really wanted to. With no obvious solution in sight, we decided to go that little bit further.

It turned out that Jackie, one of the nurses working with me the day that Mr Blake was admitted, only lived a short drive from his home. With assurance from Jackie that she would check on the dog and report back, our reluctant patient agreed to stay.

Day 2

It took a moment to figure out why Mr Blake was taking so long to get dressed — he'd pick up each item of clothing from his suitcase, hold it several inches from his face, examine it closely, and frown — but it ultimately came as no surprise when I realised that Mr Blake's eyesight was failing, and he was trying to find the least dirty shirt to put on. Everything he had was pretty bad. I distracted him with the offer of a wash, and swapped his filthy clothes for a set of hospital pyjamas.

After a steaming hot bath, a shave and a fresh set of bedclothes, Mr Blake was beginning to look a lot better. He also hadn't insisted on going home in a while. I wondered when he had last had a bath. I suspected he was starting to appreciate what he'd probably been missing for several years, maybe even for as long as his wife had been gone: a bit of TLC.

'How'd it go last night at his house?' I asked Jackie when I spotted her in the office with the charge nurse, Thabbeth. They were discussing what to do with Mr Blake.

'Well, the place really is a mess. I managed to avoid touching the dog. I'm pretty sure it has fleas. I'll go there again tonight if I have to, but we need to get something sorted out soon. I also met the neighbour, well, neighbours actually, a nice couple, young family, seemed really nice. They said they've tried to keep an eye on Mr Blake, but he generally keeps to himself.'

When I explained that Mr Blake didn't want

to bother his family, Thabbeth suggested that we should try him again. 'See if you can get his approval. I'd rather not go against his wishes.'

Technically, if a patient doesn't want his relatives to know they're in hospital, we can't do a lot, but that rule has been broken in the past, when it turns out to be the right thing to do in that instance.

Upon further questioning, it turned out that he had four children, and a decent smattering of grandchildren, some of whom he'd never even seen. But Mr Blake remained adamant that his family didn't need to know he was in hospital.

Jackie and I were not prepared to let the matter drop.

'Would you agree that your children would want to know you're here?' Jackie asked.

Mr Blake reluctantly nodded his head.

'Would they want to help you out?'

Another nod.

'Then you need to let us call them.'

Mr Blake sighed. 'You bloody well don't give up, do you, woman? But the answer is still no. No one can see me like this.' Mr Blake seemed surprised by his own words and promptly shut up, but it was too late. Everything became crystal clear; Mr Blake was too ashamed to let his family see the state he was in.

'This bloody woman knows what she's saying, Mr Blake,' I stepped in. 'They're probably going to find out at some stage anyway. You're going to be seeing some social workers, some district nurses, maybe even a cleaner to help keep the house tidy. You're going to have a whole lot of people helping you out, whether you like it or not.'

This wasn't exactly true, as we can't force help on anybody, but sometimes a little bit of exaggeration is in order.

'I'll make the call,' Mr Blake finally said.

Day 3

The events of the following day were beyond our control. Mr Blake's three daughters, two sons-in-law and a litter of grandchildren descended upon our ward. The eldest daughter introduced herself as Cathy, and told us she lived just an hour out of the city. Mr Blake's two other daughters lived about four hours away.

Cathy was horrified to find out her father had not been coping. She felt ashamed that she had no idea he was in such a state.

'It's all my fault. I do call him, every week. He tells me he's fine. I knew I should've come to see him. I'm so sorry, so sorry. He's too proud.' It was heart-wrenching — and warming — to see her love for her father. Her sentiments were echoed by everyone else in the family.

The greatest moment came when Mr Blake was introduced to his youngest grandson, Michael, for the first time. The poor man laughed and cried at once, taking the child, who must have been about five years old, in his skinny arms.

Mr Blake's family eventually left, but not before a plan of action was put in place.

337

Day 4

Meetings took place between Thabbeth, Cathy, social services, and, of course, with Mr Blake. Cathy decided to move into Mr Blake's house for the next two months, while the services were put into place that Mr Blake desperately needed.

After which, a district nurse would visit once a week and a cleaner would come every few days. Someone was arranged to do Mr Blake's laundry. Meals on wheels would be provided for his main meal of the day. Most importantly, his children promised never to listen to anything he said on the phone. Instead, they settled to take turns visiting him once a week.

As for Rascal, he wouldn't leave his best friend's side, except when the family took him to get cleaned up and had him bathed, de-flead, de-wormed, and fed a proper meal.

People in Mr Blake's situation are extremely common. They are not necessarily in need of a tablet or medical treatment, but when we take care of a patient, we look at the whole person, and try to provide complete (holistic) care.

Thankfully, we're pretty lucky that the health systems in both New Zealand and the UK do so much more than provide a place to patch up a wound, or dole out medicine.

Where am I now?

My latest adventure is not too far from London. I managed to convince a ski company in the Alps that they needed me as a nurse and ski instructor. After which, I moved on to a job as a school nurse at an elite boarding school in Switzerland, where I remain.

I never dreamt that one day I'd be a school nurse. In fact, I once looked down on school nurses as not being real nurses. But here I am wiping sniffly noses, giving out emergency contraceptives, and trying my best to help the children whose parents entrusted their kids to me.

Clinically, it's not the most demanding of jobs, but ethically, it's the biggest challenge I've faced so far.

I stay in the job because of my family. London is a great place to live when you're young and have no commitments, but with a young family to support, this job provides all I need. The hours are good, the holidays better, the pay is adequate, and although this is not New Zealand, it's still pretty darn nice.

Life might not have turned out how I expected, but I'm content, although I do feel that the kids of the rich and famous also have a few stories that need telling . . .

Acknowledgements

How do you thank the people who have made you who you are? Every nurse, doctor or patient that I can remember has left an impression on me that has affected my view of the world, of illness, of right and wrong. I guess one way in which I can say thank you is to keep on nursing, and keep on caring.

On a more pragmatic note, there are some people very close to me that I would like to thank. I do not have the words to express how grateful I am to my family, who have kept me going, and kept believing in me. A special thank you also goes out to my brother whose idea it was to start writing.

Nothing would have been possible without the support and patience of my wife. She kept me sane and kept the kids busy.

I'd also like to thank certain people at the Royal College of Nurses who helped attract the attention of a prominent publisher, as well as certain people at New Zealand's premier nursing magazine, *Kai Tiaki*.

There are countless more people to thank.

Thank you, everyone.